Groundwork
Training
for your horse

Lesley Bayley

Photography by **Bob Atkins**

David & Charles

Contents

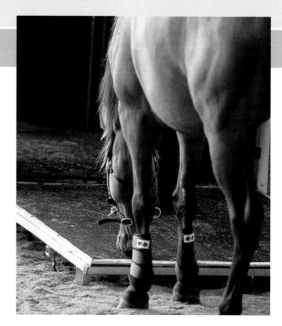

Artworks on page 119 by Maggie Raynor
Photograph on page 43 courtesy of Monty & Pat Roberts, Inc.
Photographs on pages 60–1 are courtesy of Mark Rashid

A DAVID & CHARLES BOOK

David & Charles is a subsidiary of F+W (UK) Ltd.,
an F+W Publications Inc. company

First published in the UK in 2004

Distributed in North America by F+W Publications, Inc.
4700 East Galbraith Road
Cincinnati, OH 45236
1-800-289-0963

A catalogue record for this book is available from the British Library.

ISBN 0 7153 1603 6

Printed in Singapore by KHL
for David & Charles
Brunel House   Newton Abbot   Devon

Commissioning Editor: Jane Trollope
Desk Editor: Sarah Martin
Art Editor: Sue Cleave
Project Editor: Jo Weeks
Production Controller: Jennifer Campbell

Visit our website at www.davidandcharles.co.uk

David & Charles books are available from all good bookshops;
alternatively you can contact our Orderline on (0)1626 334555
or write to us at FREEPOST EX2110, David & Charles Direct,
Newton Abbot, TQ12 4ZZ (no stamp required UK mainland).

The truth about groundwork

IT'S GOOD FOR BOTH OF YOU

Working a horse from the ground has long been a tradition in horsemanship. If you watch a display by horsemen from the established centres of excellence, such as the Spanish Riding School of Vienna or the Cadre Noir in France, you will see horses being worked in-hand and on long lines. This is an ideal way of teaching new movements to horses without them having the added burden of a rider on their back.

All kinds of disciplines have their own methods of training on the ground including:

- round pens, as used by many Western riding trainers and followers of natural horsemanship;

- lungeing, which is an integral part of many systems;

- work over ground poles, as used by many people for educational and rehabilitative purposes.

Whatever the methods used, the objective of groundwork is to produce a more confident, supple, co-ordinated horse that understands the handler's requests and can perform the required movements with ease. Once this has been achieved from the ground, the transition to ridden work is easier, as is overcoming problems such as reluctance to load into trailers and lorries.

Groundwork can be used to help horses of all ages, as a tool to teach the young horse just learning his job and to aid in the rehabilitation of horses that have become sour or frightened by life's experiences. Many people who are successful with horses use some degree of

groundwork in their training programmes, perhaps without consciously thinking about it. It is all part of the mix called horsemanship. There have always been people regarded as good horsemen and those that are not. However, until recently, horsemanship did not have any other terms prefixing it. Natural horsemanship is becoming more commonplace now but up until the late 1980s most of the horse people in Britain knew very little about it. The methods of horsemanship taught at that time – call them traditional, or normal, or what you will, were very much based on the idea that the horse was there to do a job. If he 'misbehaved', he was punished, by being told off with a slap from the whip, or being sent forwards by use of whip and spur. It was not obvious common practice to consider whether the horse was in pain or discomfort, perhaps from a back problem or an ill-fitting saddle. No doubt some horsemen and women were taking this approach, but they were not shouting about it and letting others know. Among the ordinary horse-owning and riding public, there was not a great awareness of different methods of dealing with horses.

People would depend upon gadgets or stronger bits to control hard-pulling horses, while forcing a horse into a trailer by whacking it with a broom or whip was commonplace and often recommended by the 'experts'. Physiotherapists were very much on the outside of the veterinary scene and the equine dentist

was a pretty rare breed. Then a revolution happened, and it started with the visit of an American to Britain. When Monty Roberts was invited to show his methods of starting horses at Windsor Castle in the late 1980s, the seeds of change were sown.

From this point on, the idea of learning to think like a horse to gain a better understanding of horses has snowballed. Using your body language to attract a horse's attention and manipulate his movements has become more acceptable. There may well have been trainers in the UK who were already doing this to some degree or other but it was Monty Roberts who showcased it to the general horse-owning public and gave the process a structure, which he called Join-Up.

Over time the tag of 'natural horsemanship' has been loosely applied to the work of Monty Roberts and several other trainers. The definition of the term has evolved and is discussed further on page 40.

The truth about groundwork

IT'S GOOD FOR BOTH OF YOU

Whether you love or loathe the growth of natural horsemanship, you have to admit that it has certainly got horse people thinking about and discussing these training methods. And it can only be a good thing that more people are aware that horses do have emotions, opinions and instinctive behaviour. The idea of having a real bond and partnership with a horse is more important to many people than competitive success and more people now stop and think before deciding what equipment to use on their horses. Working the horse from the ground is an essential element in many of the systems developed by natural horsemen and so has become an increasingly popular part of the ordinary owner's routine. The value of groundwork is phenomenal, as an educational tool and as a way of resolving problems, as you will see from this book. The beauty is that both horses and handlers benefit from it too!

There is no doubt that establishing a good relationship with your horse on the ground, and introducing new exercises in-hand before trying them under saddle, helps to smooth the way to success.

This book looks at various ways of working the horse from the ground, explaining the benefits of each. Look upon the methods described as an array of tools to help you get the best from your horse. Certain tools will be of use time and again, with many different horses, while other tools may be essential for one particular horse, but not necessary for another.

Horses are all individuals and should be treated as such. Whether you are working a horse

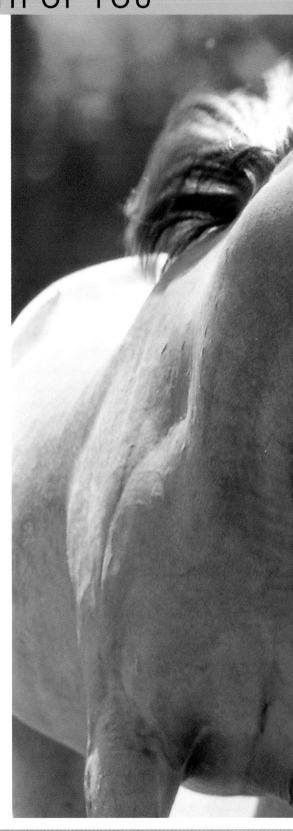

from the ground or riding, you should always listen to what he is telling you and devise his lesson for that day according to the circumstances on the day. Tomorrow may bring a different set of needs altogether and you will have to adjust accordingly.

The advantage of having a large 'tool kit' of techniques to use is that if something is not working you can quickly change to another 'tool'. Working a horse from the ground also gives you the opportunity to observe his way of going, to see whether he uses himself efficiently, and to learn from his face and body movements, whether he is finding something difficult or not.

Getting to know and understand your horse is vital if the partnership is to grow and succeed. How well do you know your horse? Do you know where he carries tension in his body? Does he stand square? Can you touch him all over his body? Does he flex both hocks evenly? On a small circle, does he take his hind leg to the midline on either rein? Does he rely on you and the lunge rein for balance when being lunged? Does he lean to one side when being led? How does this relate to his work under saddle?

If you are not sure of the answers to these questions now, you will know how all this relates to your horse once you have read this book and tried some of the exercises. As both you and your horse will discover, groundwork can be good fun as well as educational and is a great way of working the body. It also provides a solid foundation for your ridden work and can be included as a regular part of your horse's weekly training programme.

1:Know Your Horse

Basic handling techniques

WHAT YOU NEED

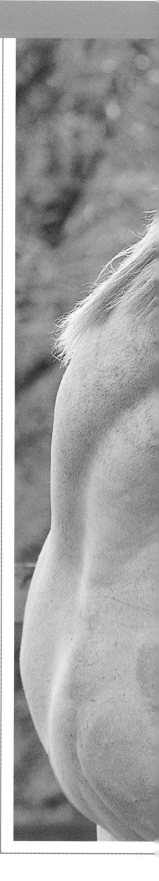

A well-mannered horse is a pleasure to own and to deal with every day. However, if you have to cope with a badly behaved animal, time with your horse becomes a chore. In addition, if you need to ask anyone to look after him while you are away, volunteers are not so forthcoming if he is known for his bad behaviour. The more problems or quirks the horse has, the more difficult it is to sell him, too.

Basic good manners are essential. So what are they?
You should be able to:

• lead your horse without him pulling away or walking over you.

• work around him in the stable without him biting or kicking you.

• tie him up without him pulling back and breaking free.

• enter the stable without having to push him out of the way or stop him barging out.

• turn him out into the field safely and catch him when required.

• touch him all over his body so that, if necessary, you can deal with wounds, administer wormers, have the vet inject or treat as necessary. Naturally horses that are in pain or discomfort will be tetchy and allowances can be made for this. However, it is sensible to get your horse used to being handled all over as this makes it easier to deal with him in times of emergency – if he has to have a stomach tube inserted, for example.

• pick up his feet easily.

• tack up and fit rugs, bandages, travelling gear, and so on without problems.

• clip him.

• load him into a trailer or lorry.

• ride him in the arena, on roads and bridleways, and deal with any hazard you meet.

• let the farrier, vet or equine dental technician do their jobs without having to worry your horse will fight them.

As the chat rooms on internet sites and advice columns in magazines indicate, there are lots of owners whose horses do not meet even these very basic requirements. Here are some pointers to help you teach your horse the basics.

Basic handling techniques

THE IMPORTANCE OF TOUCH

Horses communicate with each other in various ways, one of which is touch. They are tactile creatures and usually enjoy physical contact. Within a short time of giving birth, mares lick their foals, cleaning them but also bonding with them. Through touch foals locate their dams' udders, often with the mare giving the foal a gentle nudge in the right direction. In the early months, touch will be a regular part of life as the foal learns how to groom with his dam, seek reassurance from her presence or take chastizement with a nudge or nip.

2 Horses are also accustomed to rhythm from an early age: the mare rhythmically licks her foal's body when he is born and her tail will swish rhythmically over his face when he is at the milkbar. This acceptance of rhythm can be used in training – for instance when accustoming a horse to accept strange sensations, such as a rug on its back, or to accept tack.

1 Touch is part of a horse's world from his very first hours and it continues to be important to him throughout his life.

3 Throughout their lives, horses indulge in mutual grooming with close friends (these can include people as well). When worried, they will look to the comfort of other horses (or humans if there is a close bond). You will know how stroking can help calm a horse and how much they appreciate being scratched in certain spots.

GROOMING

Touching your horse is a vital part of getting to know and understand his body. Daily grooming is a vital part of the routine in that it:

- ensures any mud or dirt is removed prior to the horse being ridden;
- stimulates the skin, ridding it of sweat and waste products and maintaining it in good condition;
- improves muscle tone;
- stimulates blood circulation;
- improves the horse's appearance;
- provides the opportunity to check for any swellings, heat, and signs of injury.

1 There are different schools of thought on picking up a horse's hind foot. The long-accepted way is to run the hand down the inside of the horse's leg as shown.

2 Many schools of natural horsemanship advocate running the hand down the outside of the horse's leg. The foot is brought forward slightly and then taken back to a working position. This helps a horse to balance and prevents you from being kicked.

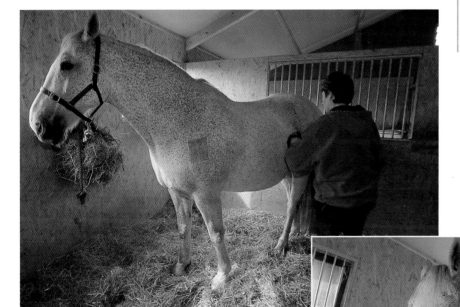

3 When grooming your horse take note of his reactions as an unwillingness to be brushed somewhere could indicate discomfort in that area.

4 Cleaning the eyes, nostrils and dock are part of the normal daily routine and are easier to do if your horse accepts being touched all over his body.

1: Know Your Horse

There are also benefits in using your hands to touch your horse's body and accustom yourself to how the skin, hair and muscles feel.

2 Make a point of running your hands slowly over your horse's body. How does his skin feel? Are there places where the skin and muscle feel tight? Can you feel knots of muscle? Note how the texture of the hair can differ, feeling quite fine in some areas and quite coarse in others. Can you feel more heat or cold in some areas? Is your horse more sensitive or wary to your touch in certain places?

1 Unless your horse is totally accepting of your touch, you will find that he is more wary in some areas – these include the neck and spine, belly and legs. These are the horse's vulnerable spots, the places where in the wild a predator might attack and cause fatal injuries. Despite thousands of years of domestication, the horse still has strong instincts to protect these areas. Do not punish a horse for being wary of being touched in these spots; instead, gently insist that contact is made and prove to him that he is not in danger.

3 When working over your horse's body, watch his responses so that you can pinpoint areas of sensitivity or concern. If you find problem areas, you can address them or call in the services of a relevant therapist to help.

FIELD MANNERS

The field is where your horse can relax, play, eat and socialize with other horses. Providing he has not had any past traumas, in this environment he will know how to relate to other horses and how to behave in equine society. He will have learned this behaviour from his dam and from interacting with other horses of all ages. He also has to learn how to behave with people in the field: just as he must respect the personal space of his fellow equines, he should respect your space. The importance of having a respect for your space is a theme common to many equine trainers, where ever they come from.

1 Before this mare had a foal she was used to being visited in her field without necessarily being caught and brought in to work. Now she has a foal at foot, she is relaxed about being visited and fussed. Her foal has also learnt that this is normal and is something to look forward to.

2 Offering a hand like this is a non-threatening gesture to a horse. With foals it may be necesssary to bend down so you are smaller and less intimidating.

3 As you can see, the foal enjoys receiving attention from a person. At this early age foals are very receptive to new experiences – from this we moved on to picking up his feet without any hassle.

4 Whenever you work your horse, whether under saddle, in-hand or on the lunge, finish off the lesson by asking him to stand in his own space. If your horse is attached to you, he may well follow you as you move away but keep halting him, telling him to stand while you move away and praising him when he remains still.

Basic handling techniques

Your horse may see his stable as his territory so be aware of how you enter it and how you behave while there. Do not just barge into your horse's stable, speak to him as you approach as he may be dozing and could easily be frightened if you suddenly appear without any advance warning. Take a little time to talk to him over the stable door and observe his behaviour – hopefully he will be receptive to your company. If he is aggressive see pages 80–87 for guidance.

1 As you open the stable door, your horse should step back to give you more room to enter. You can teach him to do this quite easily. Initially, you may have to put your hand against his chest and gently push him back as you say 'back'. When he steps back, reward him. Most horses catch on to this very quickly.

2 Be consistent with your command to 'back' and a reward so that it becomes second nature for your horse to back up when you open the stable door.

WORKING IN THE STABLE

Some horses are wary of people in their stables, often because they have had a bad experience in the past. I had a mare who was very worried by anyone in her stable: she would immediately get as far away as possible and watch the person very carefully, moving out of range all the time. We discovered that someone had beaten her in her stable. My approach was always to keep my body language and voice tone non-threatening and to move around her in a very clear, consistent way. Within a few days she was much more relaxed and within a matter of weeks she was happy to have strangers in her stable and to accept contact from people.

USING BODY LANGUAGE

People can make themselves look threatening to a horse by squaring their shoulders and drawing themselves up to their full height, puffing out their chest, looking the horse straight in the eye and holding their arms out to the sides.

You can look less threatening by rounding your shoulders, letting the 'life' go out of your body and not making eye contact with the horse.

These extremes are not often needed but do be aware of how you present yourself to your horse. You may unintentionally be making an aggressive face at him!

Often horses are aggressive out of fear – they are trying to get in the first blow because past experience has shown that they will get hit. Horses are much bigger and stronger than us, so there is little point trying to force our will on them – handlers need to use their brains and engineer situations so that the horse willingly does what we want him to do.

Do not respond to horses that kick or bite by losing your temper. If a horse aims a bite at you, use your arm and elbow to block him, making a very quick movement but not necessarily making contact. The most usual cause of this kind of behaviour is a lack of respect from the horse for the handler. To find ways to address this see Michael Peace's Think Equus approach (page 80).

① Many trainers use the pressure-and-release method to teach a horse to walk into pressure rather than pulling against it. This also prepares the horse for being tied up. Michael Peace uses an ordinary headcollar for this purpose, while other trainers use pressure halters, which exert more force. This is a simple pressure halter; the horse should not actually be tied up in a pressure halter.

② A lunge line running from the headcollar, through the tie ring to the handler is sometimes used to train a horse to be tied up. Most horses are a little concerned when they first feel the restriction of being tied up. With this method, if the horse has a fit at being restricted, the handler can let the lunge line run back through the ring and thus avoid possible injuries to the horse if it struggles.

TYING UP

All horses have to be tied up at some time – for grooming, shoeing and so on. The horse's instinct is to move – in the wild he spends much of his life on the go, and survives due to his ability to run from danger. It is not surprising therefore that horses initially find it hard to accept being tied up. However, the demands of domestic life mean that this is something the horse has to come to terms with. There are

several methods of teaching a horse to tie up, most involve the use of pressure and release. Always tie up using a piece of breakable string so the horse doesn't get injured if he panics and pulls away.

TEACHING A HORSE TO MOVE OVER

Working around a horse in a stable is much easier if the horse will move left or right on command as well as back. Our photographs were taken outside for clarity but this work is normally introduced in the stable.

Use your hand where a leg aid would be applied and combine the vocal request 'over' with pressure from the hand. Reward your horse for his effort. This technique can be used with young horses as well: it is good preparation for their work under saddle.

Basic handling techniques

LEADING

There are several ways to lead a horse. Here we show three different approaches. If a horse is difficult to lead, handlers often switch to stronger methods of restraint such as lungeing cavessons, bridles or chifneys. However, this doesn't address the basic cause of the leading problem. For instance, if a horse finds it hard to balance himself and control his body, it makes more sense to use other approaches, such as TTEAM positions, to overcome the root cause.

TIP
• When leading your horse through doors or in narrow spaces, give him enough room – if he knocks his hips you will dent his confidence as well as possibly bruise or injure him.

1 Anyone who has been taught in a British Horse Society approved school will lead a horse by positioning himself or herself alongside the horse's near shoulder.

2 Other schools of thought stress the importance of the horse learning to respect your personal space. They teach the horse to stay in his space and only come into the handler's space when invited. The handler can then position themselves ahead of and to the side of their horse in order to lead.

3 This two-person TTEAM leading position teaches horses to be handled from the offside as well as nearside and is helpful for youngsters who are finding it hard to balance, as well as older horses with balance problems. It is also useful for horses that are difficult to lead for any reason, as it gives them more to concentrate on. A 'wand' held in front of the horse teaches him to respond to his handler's signals while at a distance and encourages his self-control and confidence (see also pages 92–3).

Horses use their body position and posture, speed and direction of travel to manipulate the space and movement of other horses and people. Within a herd, a dominant member can move another horse away from food or water. With horse-human relationships, a horse can manipulate a person's movements so that they find themselves jammed against the stable wall or frantically trying to get behind the horse to send it forwards on the lunge.

1 This rider has trouble with her horse under saddle. However, you can see that the mare's eye is rolled away from her owner, showing the root of the problem – a lack of attention and respect for her space.

2 Through making constant changes of direction while leading her, the handler (Michael Peace) ensures that the horse begins to pay attention. Being able to manipulate a horse's movement shows that we are important and gives the horse a reason to look to us as leaders.

3 With the mare's attention gained, work turns to making her aware of the handler's personal space. Turns, stops and starts encourage her to follow yet maintain a respectful distance.

4 When the horse enters the handler's space, he backs her up by taking a step towards her. As soon as she moves back, the handler stops and gives her a rub as a reward. Remember, this is a powerful tool, which should be used with respect. If it is used to dominate your horse, it is hindering the partnership you are aiming to build.

DESENSITIZING – WHIP PHOBIAS

1: Know Your Horse

In their daily lives horses have to cope with many things that are alien to them – for instance, wearing rugs, being confined in small spaces that then move (ie travelling in trailers), walking up ramps, being clipped, and encountering strange objects such as pigs, cars or farm machinery.

The horse is a flight animal, and his natural instinct when faced with something he perceives as dangerous is to flee. So the introduction that a horse has to these things is crucial – get it right and the horse will accept the process for the rest of its life, get it wrong and the horse will have problems that may well affect its future.

Many owners have experienced horses whose trainers made mistakes – for instance, the horse that is not safe in traffic as it bolts whenever it meets a large vehicle, or the horse that rears and plunges whenever the clippers are switched on. To help a horse overcome fears such as these, a training process known as systematic desensitization is used. This involves exposing the horse to the thing he finds fearful but doing this progressively so that he accepts and begins to understand the situation.

It is essential that the trainer observes the horse's reactions second by second so that he is never pushed too far. If he is over-exposed to something he finds frightening, he will be even more sensitized to it, rather than de-sensitized. It may take several sessions over a week or more to accustom a horse to the clippers but this is a small amount of time considered against a horse's lifespan. Once a horse has truly accepted being clipped, loaded, shod and so on, he will be easy to clip, load and shoe for the rest of his life, unless something untoward happens, such as he has an accident in a trailer, for example.

TIPS
- If you misjudge your horse's acceptance of the whip/clippers and he reacts by pulling away then you need to go back a step. Spend time on getting the foundations right and the rest will follow.

- It is better to under-expose your horse and take longer to achieve a result than to over-expose him and risk stimulating him to such an extent that fear takes over. If the latter happens there is a risk of the horse injuring himself and you. Over-exposing or 'flooding' a horse can lead to him breaking down mentally or physically.

- You may find that dealing with one fear or phobia has an effect in other areas in that your horse's self control and confidence increases so he feels able to deal with other issues that previously worried him.

1 This sequence is designed to help a horse with a fear of whips. Before the photo session, we had run through the steps in this photo and the next one but photos 3–5 show first-time reactions. Use a lunge whip (this one splits into two) to stroke around the horse's shoulders and then closer to her head. If your horse is relaxed about this (as here), move on to stroking over the rest of her body.

② Work on both sides of the horse's body, so repeat the stroking on the offside. Stroking the whip on this mare's offside is a little more concerning for her. Look at her ears, focused back on what is happening. Most horses are used to having everything done to them on the nearside but it is important to work on the offside as well.

③ Now stroke the full-length of the whip along the horse's body, starting at the shoulder and working up and down both sides. It's important not to irritate or tickle the horse with the whip – she needs to feel a confident, constant pressure. Watch your horse as you are doing all this and use your voice for reassurance.

④ If this goes well then you can move away from the horse and flick the whip over in front of her head. This mare can be quite headshy at times but was happy with this. I stopped at this point as she had made big strides towards overcoming her fear in a very short time.

⑤ If your horse accepts full-length stroking, try flicking the whip over her body, being careful to keep everything in a consistent rhythm (remember the photo of the foal with the mare's tail flicked across his face, page 12). The rhythm is quite soothing and I am careful not to crack the whip or to let it hit her body sharply.

Basic handling techniques

1: Know Your Horse

Once a horse will accept being touched all over by hand, it's useful to introduce other sensations such as being rubbed all over with plastic. This will feel strange to the horse and there is the added dimension of the sound it makes, and this is good preparation for wearing rugs and for being ridden – for instance if the rider's coat makes a rustly noise.

Teaching a horse to accept the touch of plastic also encourages him to think first rather than act instinctively – that is, not to run away. The process is a gradual one using systematic desensitization and can be used with horses of all ages. Our equine model is the horse that was worried by whips. She tended to rush a great deal, out on hacks, towards her fences, when working on the flat, when being led to the field and so on. Getting her used to whips and working with plastic, including stepping on to plastic laid on the ground, has encouraged her to use her head and to think about situations so she is now much calmer on the flat, on hacks and in-hand. This sort of work also seems to help horses that are worried by vehicles or people coming up behind them.

1 Start off with a carrier bag and let the horse have a good sniff at it. Some horses like to get hold of it as well – let them explore it so that they know it is not going to hurt them.

2 Begin at the shoulder as this is a fairly neutral place. Rub the bag on the horse using a circular motion and observing her reaction. If your horse accepts the feel and the noise, start to work over a larger area.

3 Now work along vulnerable areas, such as the spine, belly or legs, then rub the plastic over all the body. This should only be done if your horse fully accepts the situation.

4 As the horse becomes more confident you can gradually open out the bag so that a bigger piece of plastic is being rubbed over her body. The horse's belly is often ticklish and it is also a vulnerable area – she may be inclined to kick out, so be careful here.

5 Rub the plastic up along the neck towards the poll and head. This horse took just a few minutes to reach this stage.

Over the next few days, repeat the work, getting further each day until the horse is happy to accept a much bigger piece of plastic over it, as here. Young horses are very open to new experiences and will quickly become accustomed to them, providing the lessons are introduced sensibly.

Preparing for groundwork

PHYSICAL AND MENTAL FITNESS

Before you can prepare a training programme for your horse you need to know as much as possible about him. Your hands and your eyes are your most valuable tools as through these you can learn a great deal. Earlier on (pages 10–23) the importance of touch and getting to really know your horse's body was highlighted – this should be an on-going part of his care as problems will come and go and you need to be aware of what is affecting him at any particular time. In addition, get into the habit of regularly checking things like saddle fit, as your horse may change shape, perhaps through weight gain or loss, or through muscle being built up or lost, and foot condition.

It's important to know how your horse normally moves as well – and you should compare his movement to how you would expect a horse of his type/breed/age to move. It's surprising how many youngsters I see that are very stiff or restricted in their movement, usually relating to a muscle problem, yet the owners are often unaware of it. Changes in a horse's musculature and way of moving can happen over a period of time so it's easy not to notice that things are changing until there is a problem. Get into the habit of noticing things about your horse, assessing him regularly and questioning yourself. For example, how does he feel to ride compared with last month? It does help to keep a diary in which to note your observations as it is easy to forget details. When a problem arises, you can then look back over a period of time to check for any trends or little signs which, when added together might have been the cause.

Use a diary to record your progress as well: often people fail to realize how much they have achieved over time. Photographs and video footage can also help – when you are working with a horse every day you may not see the physical changes taking place as the horse builds muscle or becomes more balanced or supple.

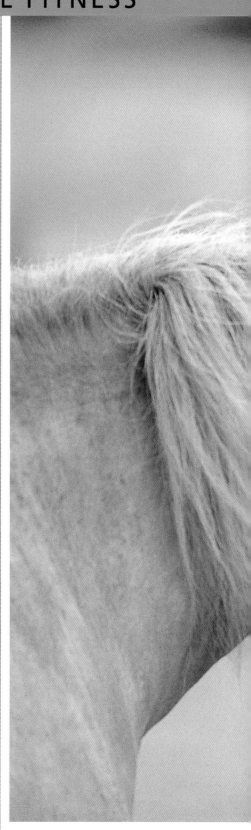

1: Know Your Horse

In addition to knowing how your horse's body feels, you need to be familiar with how he moves. This will enable you to select exercises from the variety included in this book so that you can address his individual needs.

DECIDING ON A PLAN OF ACTION

Write down your observations on your horse and keep them close to hand as you read through the different techniques described. Make notes of those ideas that you feel will be of most help. For instance:

If your horse has a habit of barging you could try:
- the Think Equus respect and attention work.
- teaching him to step back from the stable door.
- teaching him to stand in his own space.
- using the TTEAM leading techniques.

If your horse has difficulty turning on one rein you could try:
- TTEAM labyrinths.
- stretching exercises.
- calling in other help such as a physiotherapist or EMRT therapist.

If your horse finds lateral work difficult you could try:
- locating problems through touch and assessment.
- teaching him to move over and progressing to working him in-hand.
- using the Parelli Games.

1 Watch your horse being walked away from you and towards you. Does he walk in a straight line or does he hang towards the handler? Does he wander around instead of moving straight? How does he use his hips, stifle, hocks and fetlocks – do they move easily or does he look stiff? Can he flex his hocks? Does he rush? Does he move very closely behind or in front? Do any of his limbs cross in front of others or are they thrown out to the side as he moves? Does his tail swing easily from side to side or is it clamped down or held to one side? Is his stride shorter than you'd expect for his type? Watch your horse in walk and trot. Does one pace exaggerate anything?

2 Watch as your horse turns both ways when being led and as he is turned in small circles. Does he shuffle or flow around a turn? Does he look stiff? Do his hind legs come under the midline as he turns or circles? On a circle or turn is the outside hind leg lifted up and out so it takes a different track to that of the front leg?

TIPS

• You can also watch your horse on the lunge. Try him with and without his saddle. Is there any difference in his movement? Does anything you see relate to how he feels when being ridden?

Preparing for groundwork

STRETCHES AND SUPPLING EXERCISES

1: Know Your Horse

By incorporating a few simple exercises into your horse's daily routine, you can increase his mobility at the same time as preparing him for work. The routines shown here are passive suppling exercises. When combined with suppling exercises under saddle, they help to improve the horse's range and quality of movement, assisting in his overall performance.

BEFORE YOU START

- These exercises can be done with a 'cold' horse as you are not asking him to take his leg out to its maximum range, nor are you asking for a continual stretch on the tissues. However, it will make your work easier if you can walk him around a little to loosen him up before you start.
- Maintain a good posture yourself, keeping your back straight with your feet firmly on the ground so you have a good base of support and balance.
- Ensure your horse is standing square and balanced before you start the exercises.
- Work on a non-slip surface.

TIP
- Beware of lifting limbs too high or trying to take them too far forward or back. Watch your horse's ears and tail for signs of anxiety or discomfort.

1 Pick up a foot, holding it just above the ground. Slowly make small circles, three anti-clockwise and then three clockwise. Your horse may find it difficult at first but you'll see a difference within a few days. Repeat the exercise on the other legs – including the fore limbs – you may notice that your horse finds it easier on one side than the other.

2 Pick up the foot but this time take the leg slowly across to the opposite leg, again describing small circles as you go. Start off with small circles, making them progressively larger. Remember to describe the circles in both directions.

3 Now take the horse's leg out to the side, performing circles as you go. You must be aware of your horse so that you do not take his leg too far and throw him off balance. Do the circles slowly, as you take the leg out and as you return the leg to its start position.

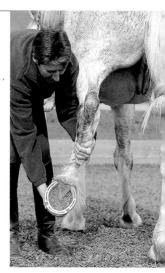

4 The next step is to take the horse's leg forward towards the front leg. You must keep the foot close to the ground and beware of taking it too far. Describe your clockwise and anti-clockwise circles as you take the leg forward.

TIP
• Remember to carry out these exercises slowly and keep them within the horse's comfort zone. Listen to your horse.

5 Slowly take the leg backwards, making the circles as you go and return to the start position. Initially your circles will be small but you can progressively work towards larger circles.

1 These stretches (above and right) are often referred to as 'carrot stretches' as carrots are the inducements offered to encourage the horse to stretch. Ask the horse to turn her head sideways to the left and then to the right to reach the carrot held towards the end of her ribcage. This horse is stiff in the neck so she has had to lower her head to reach the carrot. Massaging her neck and doing these stretches on a daily basis will help her overall mobility.

2 Then ask the horse to bend her head and neck to reach a carrot held between her front legs. She finds this difficult too. Again, daily stretches will loosen her up.

Preparing for groundwork

MASSAGE

Massage has been used on people for centuries and has become increasingly popular for horses as well. It benefits horses physically and relaxes them mentally. A good knowledge of the horse's anatomy is essential for massage. The growth of interest in the art has meant an increase in the number of books and videos available. There are also courses, some aimed specifically at people who want to help their own horses. Training for a career in massage is much more demanding and time consuming.

There are several different massage techniques and these use the flat of the hands, fingertips and elbows in various ways to achieve different objectives. Although hand-held devices for massaging are available, using these means that you receive no feedback through your hands as to how the horse is feeling.

The techniques shown here are for a hand massage to generally help relax your horse and enhance venous and lymphatic flow. Use these techniques if your horse is fit and well, as a part of his routine maintenance programme. You should not massage your horse immediately after an accident, if he has a skin infection, any other kind of illness or if he is suffering from persistent undiagnosed pain. In addition, massage should not be used on dehydrated horses, those that are 'tied up' or are colicking or over wounds.

1 Effleurage is carried out with rhythmical long slow strokes. These relax the horse and are used at the start and end of a massage. The strokes are made with one hand, two hands or alternate hands. When both hands are used, they move simultaneously. If alternate hands are used one hand will finish a stroke just as the other begins a stroke. The strokes start away from the body centre and move towards its two main collection points for venous blood, the axilla (armpit) and the groin. There is an overlap between worked areas. Be rhythmical applying a light firm pressure and always observe the horse's reactions.

- Make the surroundings and timing of the massage conducive to relaxation.

- Position yourself so that you can easily glance at your horse's head so that you can read the signs. You would expect him to relax – so you should see his head and neck lower, his eyes and ears look relaxed, his lower lip droop and his breathing rate slow down.

- Ensure the horse is tied up or being held.

- Remove any feed bowls or objects that you may trip over. Be aware of the position of water buckets.

- If the weather is cold, turn back the relevant part of the horse's rug so that you can work on him but he does not become chilled.

2 Petrissage is used once the tissue is relaxed. The horse's tissues are compressed and then released. Here the fingertips are being used in a circular motion, applying pressure and then relaxing.

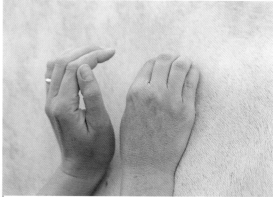

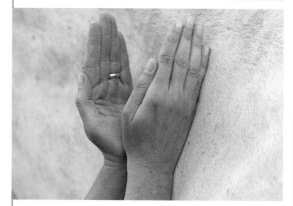

3 Clapping (top) and hacking (above) stimulate tissue, with the movements being made briskly. The hands move over the horse's body surface rapidly and are never stationary.

Preparing for groundwork

SHIATSU

Shiatsu is a very gentle system of health care that has evolved over 5000 years. It is a non-invasive hands-on form of healing which helps a wide range of problems. Shiatsu means 'finger pressure' and practitioners use their palms, fingers, thumbs and elbows on the horse's body, combined with stretches and rotations, to move and rebalance the body's vital energy or Ki (known as Chi or Qi in China).

This energy, or Ki, flows through the body via channels known as meridians. If the energy gets blocked, imbalances and eventually disease are caused. Shiatsu releases these blockages so the Ki can flow again, restoring balance and health.

1 The Bladder Meridian runs from the inside corner of the eye along the length of the horse's body (see 2) to the outer bulb of the heel of the hind foot. It is a good indicator of your horse's general state of health. At the foot fingertip pressure is applied as this is only slightly penetrating – the fingertips are very sensitive to energy.

2 The Bladder Meridian is the largest meridian in the body, covering the length of the horse. It is important for diagnosis and treatment. Here, palm pressure is being applied to move energy. The pressure is held for a number of seconds – how long depends on the sensations the practitioner feels in her hands.

3 Even headshy horses enjoy having a shiatsu treatment on their heads. Work on the jaw muscle and then on the jaw bone itself to help to reduce tension in this area.

4 Shiatsu work is performed around the bones that encircle the eye and then the eye is soothed.

5 Working on the ears helps to relieve tension at the poll. Gently rotate the ear and then apply pressure moving from the base of the ear to its tip.

The Tellington Touch Equine Awareness Method (TTEAM) was developed by Canadian trainer and horsewoman Linda Tellington Jones. Linda's training system is a combination of non-habitual movements of the horse's body, circular touches made with the hands and fingers to influence the horse's nervous system, and ground exercises to help a horse's co-ordination, balance and self-awareness. All kinds of problems can be addressed using TTEAM techniques, including loading difficulties, stiffness, short strides, high head carriage, poor co-ordination and unsteadiness when travelling.

TTEAM Bodywork is a combination of various TTEAM Ttouches on the horse's body and exercises such as leg circles (see also pages 28–9), tail circles, ear and mouth work.

TIPS

- Keep leg circles (step 6) within a comfortable range of motion for your horse. As his suppleness increases you will be able to describe larger circles.

- Do not lift your horse's legs too high if he is arthritic or has stifle problems. Tune in to your horse's reactions and work accordingly.

- Use leg circles to help horses that are reluctant to stand for the farrier. The work gives the horse more awareness of his body and improved balance.

- If your horse has problems with stride length or doing lateral work, leg circles will improve his range of motion.

- Working your horse's legs in this way helps you become more aware of stiffness or other problems before they show up as lameness.

- The circular touches must be very gentle – get the feel of them by making small circles on your eyelids without it being uncomfortable.

1 Before any TTEAM work is applied, the horse is assessed. Here, TTEAM practitioner Sarah Fisher uses the flat of her hand to detect areas on the horse's body that are sore, sensitive or tense. She also uses her fingertips, with a very light, quick-release pressure, to discover more about the level of sensitivity. The horse's reactions, such as swishing the tail, throwing the head about, moving away and so on are all noted. Sarah will also watch the horse move and turn. This information, together with what the owner has told her, will be used to devise a programme to help the horse.

2 Circular touches are used on the horse's body; made with the pads of the fingers, they actually cover a circle and a quarter and are extremely gentle. The basic Ttouch is called the Clouded Leopard and this is what Sarah is using here around the eyes. The touches help to relax the horse and reduce stress.

3 Using the Ttouches around a horse's mouth helps with overcoming issues such as biting, teeth grinding, nervousness and as preparation for worming, dental attention and bitting.

4 Working inside the horse's mouth, sliding the fingers along his gums under his upper lip, helps to change horses that are stubborn or flighty. This area is connected to the brain's emotional centre.

5 You can calm nervous or frightened horses by stroking or rubbing their ears. The Triple Heater Meridian, which affects the digestive, respiratory and reproductive systems, is found around the base of the ear while the tip of the ear has a point for shock. The ear also has other acupuncture points affecting different parts of the body. Ear work has many uses; for instance, with colic or an injury, stroking the entire ear from base to tip can alleviate pain and keep the horse out of shock.

6 Do leg circles with both the hind and fore legs to improve a horse's balance and stride and relax the muscles of the neck, shoulders, back and hindquarters. Start off with small circles, circling the hoof in both directions evenly, until you reach the ground. As you reach the ground do another circle and then place the toe on the ground instead of putting the hoof down. Resting the toe may be difficult for your horse at first, especially if he is tight in the shoulder.

7 The tail is a prime indicator for he health of the back – a soft swinging tail means a supple back. Circle the tail, in both directions, to help to relieve tension and relax the back. Circular Ttouches are used around the top of the tail and down the buttocks to aid relaxation before the tail is circled. Tail pulls apply gentle traction to the tail. Working on the tail is useful if your horse is wary of movement or noise behind him, or if tends to kick out at other horses, at his stable wall or trailer.

Case Study: A Dipped Back

THE BENEFITS OF GROUNDWORK

Lady's natural talents as a show jumper and cross-country horse meant that her teenage owner concentrated on jumping rather than working the mare on the flat. Consequently, Lady never really developed the muscles along her topline. The effects of this came to the fore a few years later once Lady had produced a couple of foals and had reached her late teens. Her back was much more dipped than would generally be expected because of the poor musculature along her topline and her slack abdominal muscles.

By now her owner was away at college and the mare was on loan. Her new rider sought help from a therapist friend and together they compiled a plan involving massage, suppling exercises, in-hand work (pages 134–47) and long-reining (pages 126–31). Massage and stretching helped her overall mobility and suppleness and also helped her to relax, while the in-hand work encouraged Lady to use her body properly so that her musculature developed.

Lady was massaged twice a week. Massage may be performed more often but her owner had time constraints. After each massage, passive stretching of the fore and hind limbs (see pages 28–9) was used. This helped Lady's mobility and circulation so that she found her in-hand work easier. Performing walk turn on the forehand and other lateral work such as shoulder-in and travers helped to strengthen her over the lumbar area, open up her shoulders and develop her hindquarter muscles. Long-reining assisted in the symmetrical development of her muscle

but also filled in the gaps in Lady's flatwork education.

Lady gradually became stronger over her back and her abdominals were more toned so she did not look as dipped. By the time she was strong enough to be ridden again, she was able to work calmly in an outline for short periods.

It is important to realize that older horses have limitations and you cannot expect them to do the work they did as youngsters. However, by using common sense and a variety of techniques, you can ensure they have happier and more comfortable lives. Lady's rehabilitation took several months and she continues to have weekly massages. As she is an older horse, her rider uses the passive suppling exercises as a precursor to ridden work.

Initially, when Lady was started on her programme there was a marked difference between her off and near sides. Now, with regular exercise therapy she feels much more even, as well as generally being more supple. Her weight is monitored regularly and the saddle fit checked monthly. After the first few months of work Lady changed shape as some of the muscle wastage around her withers was reversed, necessitating a change of saddle.

Now in her mid-20s Lady continues in light work, three or four times a week, which suits her and adds interest to her life. She is a forward-going and lively ride; onlookers are often surprised to learn her age.

1 Massage and exercises such as carrot stretches (see page 29) and passive suppling work improve mobility while also being enjoyable for the horse.

2 Long-reining allows you to develop a horse's musculature.

3 Walk turn on the forehand assists in strengthening a horse over the loins.

2: Groundwork in Practice

The Right Mix

ACHIEVING GOOD HORSEMANSHIP

Since the late 1980's natural horsemanship has grown in popularity and acceptance. However, ask anyone to define natural horsemanship and you'll get a variety of answers. To some people it means considering how horses use their body language to communicate with each other and making use of this. Others regard natural horsemanship as the use of completely different equipment such as rope halters and no bits or keeping the horse as naturally as possible, living out, without shoes and without rugs. While some follow natural methods whole-heartedly, others mix elements of the natural way, such as a greater understanding of equine psychology and communication, with their more traditional methods.

Various techniques are presented in this section. Some of you will regard certain aspects as being 'natural', other people will see them as good horsemanship, or as sensible practice marketed to appeal to our modern brand-aware society. Whatever your take on the situation it's best to look at everything in the light of how it might benefit your horse. Any technique if applied badly or to excess can have negative effects. You can dent a horse's confidence, confuse him and affect his movement, if you try to work him through trotting poles placed too close together, or lunge him in a badly-fitted and inappropriate gadget. You can bore a horse and cause him to switch off by needless repetition of a natural horsemanship game or technique. If your horse's eyes show that 'the light is on but no one is at home' you have gone too far.

When you work a horse you need to think before, during and after the event. Thinking before enables you to weigh up the situation and choose the most appropriate tool for the job. Thinking and observing when working your horse helps you see, analyse and understand his reactions as well as anticipate problems. Analysing the session afterwards builds your understanding. Applying this approach will help you to become a good horseman. Whether you take the traditional or the natural route, or a combination of both, the aim should be to become a good horseman who truly treats each horse as an individual. Good horsemanship means being fair and consistent with the horse at all times, having empathy and keeping your cool in all situations. There is no place for losing your temper, for in doing that you lose your ability to think rationally and the end result is often an over-the-top reaction, from which the horse suffers.

Understanding Equus

Monty Roberts is the American credited with introducing Britain to what is now known as natural horsemanship. It was in the late 1980s that this former champion rodeo rider was invited to Windsor Castle by the Queen to demonstrate his way of 'starting' horses. From that point on, Monty's methods have gained in popularity in the UK and his name is now part of the British equestrian scene. Well-known trainers such as Kelly Marks, one of Monty's star students, and Richard Maxwell have promoted his work.

Monty has started over 12,000 horses and he has fine-tuned his techniques through observing horses in the wild and how they interact with each other. An understanding of horse psychology and equine communication together with a healthy dose of common sense underpin his methods.

Join-Up was developed by Monty to create a bond with a horse, based upon trust, the horse and handler communicating in the language of Equus. (See pages 50–55, for an insight into Join-Up.) During Join-Up, as with all of Monty's work, the trainer rewards the horse for doing the right thing; he does not wait for the horse to do the wrong thing so that he can punish it.

Although discipline has a place in the process of Join-Up, it comes in the form of work not pain: if a horse stops paying attention to the trainer, he may be sent out to the edge of the round pen to complete a couple more laps, for example.

Monty says his life's goal is to leave the world a better place than he found it for horses and people alike. Students of Monty's work learn that their personal development plays a key part in their progress towards becoming better horsemen and women. They also learn to take responsibility for their own actions and to keep an open mind. They have to acknowledge their own responsibilities rather than blaming the horse. If your horse is not doing as you ask, look at how you are asking, what you are asking and why. What could you do to improve the lines of communication?

In order to work effectively with horses, Monty believes that the students have to learn to control their anxieties – they must be calm if they expect the horse to be calm. They also have to overcome the fear of failure and realize that a mistake provides an opportunity for learning. Another lesson is to try not to make the same mistake again.

Horses, like people, learn from their mistakes so they too must be allowed to make them. However, making a mistake does not mean a horse is stupid. If horses were stupid they would not have survived for thousands of years! Labelling horses in this way is something humans do – and by doing this you are giving yourself little chance of solving a problem.

In Britain, many horse lovers have been helped by Kelly Marks who set up the Intelligent Horsemanship Association, which runs courses in Monty's techniques.

TIPS

- If you hit a problem look at the whole picture before working out a plan of action.
- Choice is important – ensure your horse has freedom of choice. If he is coerced into something he will never be fully committed to it.
- Make it comfortable for the horse when he's doing what you want and uncomfortable when he's doing what you don't want him to do. Uncomfortable does not mean inflicting pain on the horse.
- Remember pain is a bad teacher.
- Resentment and fear prevent a horse from learning.
- When teaching a horse, it's often on the third time of asking that he understands what you want.

Monty Roberts first introduced horse people in the UK to the idea of communicating with horses via body language based on how horses interact with each other.

Intelligent Horsemanship

FOUNDATION EXERCISES

Before meeting Monty Roberts, Kelly Marks was a champion junior show jumper and a leading lady jockey on the flat and over jumps. Following his success in Britain, Monty asked Kelly to set up some courses in his methods and the result was the Intelligent Horsemanship Association. Monty says, 'I could not recommend a better teacher of my methods anywhere in the world than Kelly Marks.'

Intelligent Horsemanship was founded with the objective of bringing together the world's best horsemanship ideas to promote understanding and fair treatment of horses. Anyone interested in horses can join the association. A wide range of courses is offered and can lead to professional qualifications, or can be done purely for the individual's personal development.

Our photos show Intelligent Horsemanship instructors with students on the third day of their five-day Foundation course.

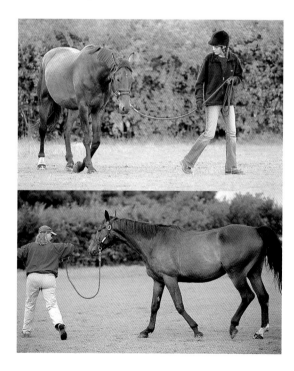

GETTING STARTED

The foundation exercises are central to working successfully with your horse as they ensure he respects you and your requests. Through them you learn to manoeuvre the horse and thus show that you are an important part of his environment, which will change his attitude towards you. In the wild, there is only one way a horse can show leadership over another and that is to move it around. You can see this happening in a paddock when one horse is at the water trough and a more dominant horse comes along; the dominant horse can easily move the other horse away, perhaps by laying back his ears or thrusting his head forward.

You want the horse to see you as a leader he can trust, not as someone aggressive to be avoided. To achieve this you must be very clear in your instructions to him. There should be no mistaking your 'yes' from your 'no'. The pressure-and-release technique helps in this communication. Intelligent Horsemanship followers often use the Dually halter designed by Monty Roberts to train their horses in pressure-and-release. The Dually looks like a headcollar except for an additional section across the nose. This has rings attached at either end so that it can be used to apply a little pressure, which is instantly released the moment the horse complies with a request. A Dually gives a little bit of extra control and the broad webbing makes it comfortable.

The timing of the pressure-and-release is crucial. Practise on a person as they can provide feedback on your handling skills.

ASKING YOUR HORSE TO COME FORWARD

This exercise asks for the horse to come toward you from a distance of at least 3m (10ft) away. Start off by being at a 45 degree angle to him and gradually bring him in towards you by applying a little pressure on the rope and releasing it the instant he shows any attempt to move. Keep your body language soft and don't have direct eye contact with him but be aware at all times of your horse's responses. Move to the side a little more if he does not respond, so that the angle is more acute. In time he will learn to respond to your body language in that if you step away, with your arms together and your eyes lowered, he will step towards you.

L-SHAPE EXERCISE – WALKING THROUGH POLES

1 Walking forwards through an L-shape of poles tests the control of both horse and handler. Students learn to do this before attempting to go backwards through it.

2 The secret is to ask the horse to take only one or two steps at a time so that you can influence where he puts his feet – providing he is paying attention!

3 Teach your horse to stop when you raise your hands as this also teaches him about respecting your personal space. Signals are given by a light feel on the rope and by the use of body language.

FOUNDATION EXERCISES

BACKING UP

Only when you are confident with moving forwards through the poles and being able to position the horse where you want him, should you try backing through the L-shape. You can see from the first attempt shown opposite that it is not as easy as you might think. (See page 48-9 for more details.) Stand in front but slightly to the side of your horse. Step towards him applying a series of short pushes on the rope, held directly underneath the headcollar. Apply the pressure on the rope until he takes a step back, as he complies, stop pushing and reward him for his effort. Just ask for one step at a time at first – and don't expect him to be able to back up in a straight line.

When the horse has learnt to back up on request, you can take the exercise to another level. Stand at least 4m (12ft) away and directly in front of your horse, looking straight at him. Raise your arms and take a small step towards him. If he steps back that's great, that is what you want. If he doesn't, shake the rope from side to side until he does step back, at which point immediately stop shaking the rope. When your horse is good at this, gradually increase the distance between you.

MOVING YOUR HORSE LATERALLY

Ask your horse to take a few steps sideways by applying light pressure from your hand in the area where a rider's leg aid would be used. If he does not respond, increase the pressure until he does. As soon as the horse moves, remove the pressure and reward him by stroking him or giving him a rub on the head so that he knows he is doing the right thing. Work from both sides. This helps with ridden lateral work and also with manoeuvring a horse in a lorry or stable.

STANDING STILL

Some horses find it difficult to just stand still and relax. Help your horse to understand the benefits of just being quiet by asking him to stand still. If he moves, quietly move him back to his original position. If your horse is very active, use this by circling him or getting him to move backwards and forwards before once again asking him to stand. It does not take a horse long to realize that moving around is hard work so he will soon choose the standing still option. The secret is not to allow yourself to get uptight if your horse is fidgety – take the energy out of your body and relax so that your horse can mimic you.

TOUCHING YOUR HORSE

Your horse should be accepting of touch all over his body and enjoy being stroked all over. If your horse does not like being touched his sensitiity could be due to pain or discomfort or simply because he is not used to being touched everywhere. Horse that do not like being groomed or tacked up often have areas of discomfort – TTEAM circles, massage or a therapy like Equine Muscle Release Therapy can all assist here. Remember that a horse in pain or discomfort is not in the best frame of mind to learn so you need to deal with this issue before moving on to other exercises.

BACKING UP THROUGH THE L-SHAPE

1 Ensure your horse is straight before you ask for a step back.

2 Here the horse is drifting off to his right. This can be corrected by moving him forwards for a step or two and then reversing again. Check your body position and your signal on the rope as you may be pushing him off to one side.

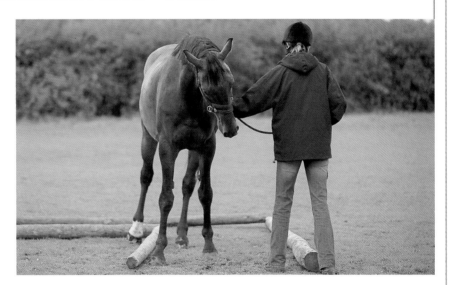

3 If you get into a muddle around the turn, stop, take a deep breath, bring the horse forwards a couple of steps and try again. Don't try to rush things. Observe how horses move so that you know which leg will move next.

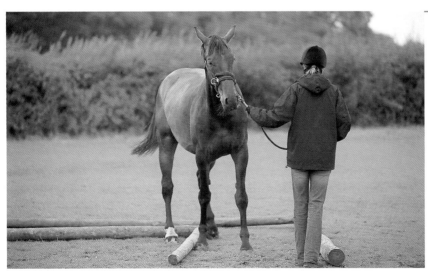

Intelligent Horsemanship

MOVING FORWARDS AND BACKWARDS THROUGH AN L-SHAPE OF POLES

Backing your horse through an L-shape made with poles tests your control of your horse's movements, his responsiveness and your mutual trust.

Start off by leading the horse forwards through the poles, walking backwards yourself and asking him to move only one or two steps at a time. Raising your arms helps to stop him and keep him out of your space.

Break down the exercise into small chunks. Once your horse is happy going forward through the whole L-shape, take him forward into it for just a few steps and then ask him to back up. If you master this you can move onto the more difficult part, negotiating the corner. Don't try to rush – take things slowly so that both you and your horse can work out the best way to get round it. If necessary you can ask the horse to go forwards, backwards or sideways if you get stuck.

Horses may step out of the poles or be wary of reversing in case they hit a pole. If it's the latter gently insist that they step back. If everything gets into a muddle, stop, get your thoughts together, stay calm and start again.

Many horses and people find this exercise difficult but with practice both horse and handler will be able to master it. Both parties need to focus their minds on the task so don't work at the exercise for more than 15 minutes at a time, otherwise your horse may well lose interest and concentration.

1 Linda, one of the instructors of Intelligent Horsemanship shows the students how to use body language to gain this horse's attention and direct his movement.

2 She stops the horse and keeps him out of her space by raising her hands.

3 She shows how to give the horse plenty of room while still being able to direct his movement.

④ Now, she moves into the centre of the poles showing the horse where she wants him to go.

⑤ A good halt – now she's preparing to back through the exercise. Inset: note her light hold on the rope, the open fingers ensure there will be no tension transmitted down the rope to the horse's head.

Intelligent Horsemanship

THE JOIN-UP PROCESS

Join-Up is the phrase Monty Roberts uses to describe the process that results in a horse indicating that he wants to be with you and chooses to stay with you as you move around. Before attempting Join-Up with a horse, it is vital that the horse is really comfortable with all the foundation exercises (see pages 44–9). Our students are working in a round pen about 15m (50ft) in diameter, which is ideal. However, you can improvise using jump poles to section off part of an arena, remembering to round off the corners so the horse does not get stuck in them.

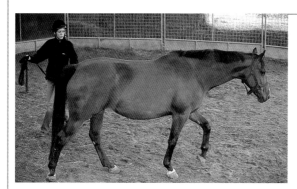

1 Join-Up starts by the horse being brought into the pen, unclipped and then 'sent away' from the handler. Here you can see the handler preparing to send the horse away by stepping behind him so that she's at a 45 degree angle to him. She keeps her shoulders square and maintains eye contact. By moving her arms up and down she encourages the horse to move off.

2 The horse is kept moving for five or six circuits of the pen. He should be going forwards freely but fairly calmly. If he is being lazy he can be encouraged to move on. The handler does this by throwing the line out behind him or by making other jerky movements, such as scuffing her feet along the ground or slapping the coiled up lunge line on her arm. The amount of pressure she puts on the horse determines the speed at which he goes round the pen, so she has to read the situation carefully.

3 Here the horse is starting to show signs that he would like to Join-Up, his inside ear is locked on to the handler in the middle of the pen, showing that he is giving her his respect and attention. Other signs of Join-Up include the horse making the circle smaller of his own accord so that he gets closer to the person, a relaxing of the head and neck, which can progress to a distinct lowering of the head, and licking and chewing.

6 Join-Up helps to create a bond of trust between horse and handler. After the Join-Up process, our student touches the horse all over his body including the vulnerable areas like the poll, neck and withers, back, belly and legs – all the places that a predator would aim for when trying to bring down a horse in the wild.

4 Seeing these signs, the handler starts to invite the horse in to her. She has to choose the spot carefully: it is harder for a horse to be drawn in from near the pen entrance or from an area where there are distractions, such as spectators. When the horse starts to give signals that he is ready to Join-Up, the student notes which area of the pen the horse is in when he gives most of his signals. This is a good place to start to draw him in.

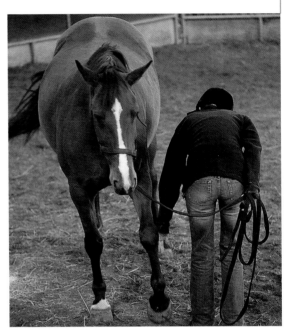

5 The student coils up her line and when the horse reaches that spot she lowers her eyes, softens her body and moves quietly away from him so that she's at a 45 degree angle in front of him. You can see how she's folded in her arm, rounded her shoulders and taken the energy out of her body. She stops, giving the horse the chance to walk up to her. When he does, she gives him a rub on the head and then walks a small circle to the right. The horse follows and is rewarded with a rub. A left circle is then completed (see pages 52–3) and the horse is again rewarded.

TIPS
- It's very important that your instructions are clear to the horse so make your body language definite.

- Be conscious of where the horse is at all times.

- When asking your horse in to you, be aware of your body language – you do not want to inadvertently block his path to you.

- If your horse gets 'stuck' on the edge of the pen rather than coming in to you, walk away in an arc shape to draw him in. Do this confidently. He will not follow you if he does not see you as the leader.

- When working over the vulnerable areas hold the line in the hand nearest the horse's head and give him confident strokes with the other hand. Kelly has a saying: 'Every compassionate hand is a healing hand.'

- Firm definite strokes help to calm a horse. Use this time to also learn about their body – how they react to being touched in the saddle area and so on.

CHANGING DIRECTION

During the Join-Up process, the horse is worked on both reins.

1 Here is another student whose horse is a little disrespectful – she throws out the line to encourage him to move on more. Note how the students are wearing jackets – this is so that if they need to slap the coiled-up line against their bodies the effect will be to make quite a noise, another aid in sending the horse on.

2 Having worked on one rein, the horse is asked to change directions. Being able to dictate the horse's direction shows that you can manipulate his movement and so are important in his hierarchy (remember how the dominant horse in the herd can direct the movement of other horses). As with all training the horse needs to work on both reins and see you (and everything else) out of both eyes.

3 Having decided on the best place to make the change of direction, the student steps across in front of the horse to effectively block his movement. To reinforce her message she maintains aggressive body language and keeps eye contact with him.

4 The hand in which she has the coiled-up line is also raised to reinforce the blocking off of one direction, so encouraging the horse to turn.

TIPS

- Join-Up is a starting point in your horse's training and your relationship with him but should not be done endlessly. Once the bond has been established through Join-Up, there's little point in going over the same ground time and again. You might use Join-Up say four times when starting a young horse. If a problem arises later you could use Join-Up once to re-establish your relationship.

- Join-Up looks easy when done by an experienced person and, as these students demonstrate, with instruction, it can be done relatively easily. However, these students have been shown the signs to look for. Inexperienced people may misread or miss entirely the subtle signs that horses exhibit.

- A formal Join-Up should take only a few minutes. If you have been working in the pen for more than six minutes then you should stop and seek expert help.

- Your body position, body language and your intent are vital elements in achieving Join-Up.

- The purpose of Join-Up is to show the horse that being with you is comfortable – so there is no place for inflicting pain or venting your frustration if things are not going to plan.

- Join-Up should not be attempted unless your horse is quiet, well-handled and can do the foundation exercises. Do not attempt this work with very young or aggressive horses (leave these to the experts).

5 The horse should make five or six circuits in the new direction …

6 … before the handler makes it easy for him to be with her and invites him in to the centre.

Intelligent Horsemanship

2: Groundwork in Practice

INTRODUCING TACK

Join-Up is often used in the starting of a young horse, to help create a bond and increase trust. After Join-Up, tack is introduced and the youngster is worked on the long-lines. With a genuine young horse, this will take some time, the lesson moving on only once he fully understands and accepts each stage. The horses shown here are already started, so these students can be taught how to introduce tack and long-line without the risk of moving on too quickly for the horse.

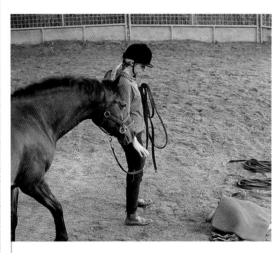

1 Everything that is required is laid out in the middle of the round pen. The horse is led past so that he can see everything from one eye…

2 …and is then led past from the other direction so that he can see the objects from the other eye. It is important that this is done otherwise he may suddenly be surprised when he changes direction and sees the tack. It also allows the handler to line up the horse so that everything is within easy reach.

3 The saddle is put on. With a genuine young horse allow him to sniff and see the saddle before putting it on. Everything is done in a relaxed, confident and rhythmic way. Horses soon pick up on their handler's worries so being able to control your emotions is essential.

4 A breastplate is attached for extra security so there is no danger of the saddle slipping too far back and scaring the horse as he works.

5 The horse is now allowed to move freely in both directions so he gets used to the feel of the saddle on his back. This step is vital in the education of young horses as if they do not truly accept the saddle of their own volition, trouble can result later (perhaps showing up as bucking under saddle or behaving badly as the rider tries to mount).

6 After a few circuits the horse is invited in – this allows for the long-lines to be attached and also acts as a reminder to the horse that the handler is a comfort zone and can be relied upon.

7 The long-lines are attached. With a young horse and with any older horse that has not been long-lined, the horse will first be accustomed to the feel of the lines and will be taught to follow the pressure of the line.

8 Long-lining in the pen – the shape of the pen helps to guide the horse round and it's important to work on both reins. The change of direction – the horse turns away from you – is achieved by stepping out in front of his movement ...

9 ... and at the same time introducing a feel in the opposite side of his mouth. The experts make it look easy but it takes time to master; here, the left rein could be looser after the turn (below).

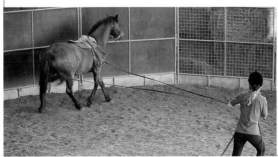

Case Study: A Problem Loader

2: Groundwork in Practice

Working a horse through the foundation exercises often removes lot of 'problems' as Intelligent Horsemanship students will testify. When faced with a problem, you need to determine the real underlying facts – do not just look at the symptoms but find the root cause. Let's take the example of this horse who was extremely reluctant to get into a horse trailer. There might have been many reasons for this:

- he had a bad travelling experience (too many drivers travel too fast!);
- he was involved in a trailer accident;
- he was beaten into a trailer and so had unhappy memories;
- he was never taught to load – or even to lead;
- he was hurt when being loaded in the past, perhaps by hitting his head on the trailer;
- he finds the trailer to be a dark and uninviting place;
- a combination of several of these factors.

Often such a problem can be made worse by the owner's behaviour – if you expect your horse to misbehave you're probably tense and displaying anxious body language yourself. He will be sensing this and feeling even more anxious himself. You may also be inadvertently blocking his way into the trailer with your own body. Be aware of this – and make a conscious effort to keep out of your horse's way and to stay calm when you are loading him. You can also change things like opening up the front unload ramp on the trailer to make the inside as light and airy as possible.

Before an attempt is made to load the horse, he is taken through the foundation exercises and he is also trained to walk over a tarpaulin laid on the ground (see right) and to walk over wooden bridges. To help him deal with anxieties such as being worried by the height of the trailer roof, he is taught to walk under plastic suspended in the air.

1 Place a sheet of plastic, secured with jump poles, on the ground. Allow the horse to use his senses – let him sniff or touch the plastic. This is his way of discovering whether the plastic poses a threat or not.

2 Taking the first steps on – allow the horse to go at his own pace and do not force him to move until he is ready. He may rush – but as he becomes more familiar with the plastic he will be less fearful.

3 This horse moves slowly onto and over the plastic, sniffing as he goes.

4 If your horse wants to stop and experience this new sensation then let him. He's learning at his own pace.

GAINING RESPECT

Many so-called 'problem' horses are simply confused because they don't know what is required and have to make a guess: if they guess incorrectly they may be reprimanded but won't know why. This leads to resentment and inappropriate behaviour. The handler must establish that he or she is a leader that the horse can trust using the leading exercise below.

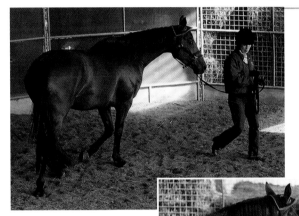

1 Kelly begins by leading the horse and starting to build a bond and trust through some simple foundation techniques. This work helps to focus the horse's attention on Kelly rather than outside influences.

2 Note Kelly's soft body language and the calm horse.

3 Even when unclipped from the lead rope, this horse is happy to follow Kelly and stay in the comfort zone beside her.

4 Testing the relationship a little more – Kelly makes lots of turns and changes of direction.

Case Study: A Problem Loader

CRUNCH TIME

Once the horse is well versed in the foundation exercises and used to going over and/or under plastic, over wooden bridges and so on, it's time to go for the real thing. It's worth doing some of your preliminary work in the vicinity of the trailer so that your horse is accustomed to working calmly around the trailer. On the day you decide to try loading, do some foundation work around the trailer first. Kelly parks the trailer so that it is part of the round pen to make it easier for the horse. Fence panels can be used alongside the ramp so the horse has fewer options for avoiding going into the trailer.

TIPS

- Practise controlling your horse's movement – it's important to be able to move each foot on request.
- Be aware of the position of your horse's head. If it is too high he will not be able to see properly. There is also the danger of his head hitting the trailer roof.
- If your horse goes off the side of the ramp don't worry, just load him from the side.
- Be confident and calm so your horse is too.
- Constantly assess and evaluate what you are doing – if something isn't working then change it.
- The aim is to give the horse a positive experience.

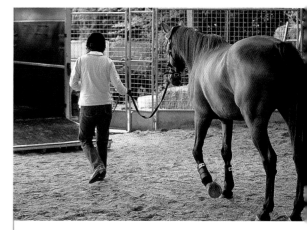

1 Approaching the ramp – note the looseness in the rope. Hanging on tightly or pulling the horse along will not work!

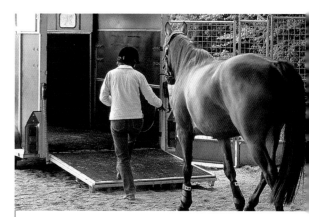

2 The handler has to control their emotions. Note how Kelly's body language is soft and passive. Her relaxed attitude helps – this is a contrast to how many people approach horses that are known as bad loaders. She keeps to the side of the horse so he can see what he has to do.

3 Allow your horse time to check everything out – it's his strong sense of survival coming into play here.

4 The horse has to keep focused on the job in hand. Pressure-and-release is used to reward him when he does the right thing and moves into the trailer. The pressure-and-release needs to be very elastic so that the instant the horse shows an inclination to move towards the pressure, it can be released.

5 Kelly makes sure that the loading is not at all confrontational. If you pull too hard there's the risk that the horse will rear and possibly hurt himself and you. The more relaxed you are the more relaxed your horse will be – it's a good idea to sigh to let go of your tension.

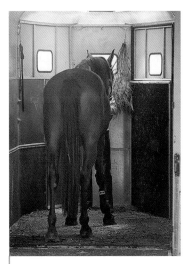

6 Once the horse is inside, Kelly rewards him as she wants the experience to have pleasant associations. You can have a handler outside the groom's door ready to pass in some food if you like. This person can also be helpful in an emergency.

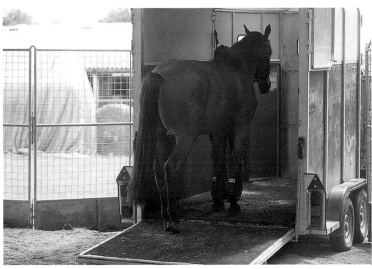

7 Kelly backs the horse out slowly. This is where it's helpful to be able to manipulate his movement and ask him to move one foot at a time. Time spent backing through the L-shape of poles pays dividends here. Don't panic if your horse goes out quickly – he will start to slow down when he realizes there is no need for him to be anxious. Repeat the loading and unloading process six or seven times in the same session to ensure he is comfortable about the whole experience.

Passive Leadership

CONSIDERING THE HORSE

Although not as well-known in Britain as some of his compatriots, Mark Rashid is attracting a growing following. He regards himself as a 'facilitator' rather than an instructor and his philosophy of 'considering the horse' has a life-changing impact upon many students. He is in the minority in offering one-on-one instruction in his clinics and he also has a different viewpoint to many, preferring what he calls 'passive leadership' to the idea of the dominant, or alpha, horse.

Mark's view is that the alpha horse maintains his position by force and through making other members of the herd expend energy in having to move away from him. On the other hand, the passive leader is usually a middle-ranking older horse who inspires the other horses to follow him by example. This passive leader is consistent in his behaviour, day-to-day, and other members of the herd follow his example willingly. In doing so, they expend less energy and so have the vital reserves if an emergency arises. In Mark's opinion, it makes sense for the horses to ally themselves to a passive leader as his attitude helps to ensure their survival.

The key attributes of a passive equine leader are consistency, dependability and leading by example. Mark bases his training philosophy on these attributes. He asks horses to do things and helps them learn how to do things without being threatening or intimidating. He teaches that good observation and clear

signals are vital if we want horses to follow us and willingly perform the tasks we ask of them.

Students who work with Mark learn to assess the situation from the horse's point of view, to listen to their horse and to be aware of how their own behaviour will affect him. They learn that by considering the horse, listening to the horse and behaving consistently, they will earn his trust. Once a horse trusts us, the possibilities are endless. One student wrote that before she met Mark she had lots of knowledge but no wisdom. Her experience with her horse at a Rashid clinic changed the way she saw and thought about her horse: instead of thinking that she owned a problem-ridden animal that she wanted to sell, she realized that all the time her horse had been telling her what was wrong. At the clinic she learned how to listen.

Another student wrote, 'Mark has a lovely quiet approach to the horse and each horse he worked with was very relaxed in his care. His voice was never raised and his requests to the horse were clear and consistent: 'asking' not 'making' being very apparent. He also has seemingly endless patience and spent the time necessary with each horse to help address the problem. I also liked the fact that there were no gimmicks or special tools of the trade. He uses the basic gear we all have and made it clear that tools are not the trick to get the horse to do something, what you do is.'

Mark Rashid's work is based on his belief that horses respond best to a passive leader. Here he is helping the young colt to learn without being threatened or intimidated. Consistent behaviour, on a day-to-day basis, provides a solid foundation from which you can become a leader for your horse.

Equine Communication

THE POWER OF POSITIVE THOUGHT

Canada's top equine behaviourist Dan Franklin has a unique approach to horses. He teaches people how to connect intuitively with their horses, initially through work on the ground, and he shows how developing this through handling and riding will be beneficial.

After years of studying horses in their own environment, Dan has concluded that they do read body language, but that this is only about 25 per cent of their communication. The other 75 per cent is achieved through the horse intuitively picking up on thoughts. Every action has to start with a thought and he believes that horses can tune in to the thought well before they read the body language that results in the action.

When communicating with each other, horses use very positive, direct but soft language. 'Horses have to think positive because if they think a negative thought they are dead,' Dan explains. Humans have a negative aggressive language. Herein lies the basis for the conflict and confusion so often seen.

Everything in the universe has energy – we all have a magnetic energy field – and this should be balanced. Often people are out of balance and horses, being highly sensitive creatures, are immediately aware of this. 'Most of the time, the problem is not about the horse but about the owner because the horse will pick up and reflect their thoughts. The horse is a total reflection of how a person presents himself or herself to a horse. That's how people get hurt, because the horse reflects their anxiety. What I do is allow people to change things within themselves. I can show

people in less than 15 minutes how powerful thought is,' he says.

Dan deals with all kinds of problem horses from those that bite, kick, won't load, and so on, to others that have shut down mentally. He watches how a horse and its rider interact and often finds that there are basic communication issues. Many horses and riders are not mentally connected and any problems are compounded when they are not physically connected either, perhaps because the rider doubts herself or is anxious about her horse's behaviour.

To help people make a better connection with their horses, Dan shows them how to work the horse from the ground. He uses a rope halter and a 4m (12ft) leadrope and plays circle games with the horse because 'horses walk in circles and zig zags not straight lines'. Through intuitive thought and a small helping of body language, Dan works with the horses to gain their confidence and trust. He then shows the owners how to do the same and helps them to use the power of thought to achieve transitions and turns on the ground.

'No-one else is teaching intuitive language yet it's so simple and everyone can do it,' says Dan. There's no doubt that he has tremendous love and empathy for horses – he has spent years and travelled the world studying them. 'Horses have become my best teachers – they have opened my mind and given me positive energy through the power of thought. I don't class myself as a healer but some people do. I say I am bringing life back into horses. I say to people coming to my clinics, "Please come with an open mind; the horses do."'

Equine Communication

1 This sequence shows Dan using the power of positive thought to tune into this horse's channels of communication.

2 Within a stride, the horse goes from trotting around Dan on a loose rope to walking. Intuitive visualization is the key.

3 When backing up the horse Dan uses a little body language but the majority of his work is based upon positive intent. He says every action has to start with a thought and horses are very good at tuning in to your thoughts. He always starts working with a horse on the ground so that he can see where the horse is at that particular moment.

4 Horses certainly want to spend time with Dan – even when loose this horse follows him, keeping close by his shoulder. Note how his head is lowered and how relaxed he is. It's even more remarkable when you learn that this horse has a history of not liking men at all! Both Dan and the horse have a soft energy here. If Dan wants to increase the mental pressure upon a horse he does so, as horses do upon each other. The ultimate aim though is to use the least amount of pressure to gain the softest feel.

5 Dan uses circles and arcs a great deal when working with horses. This is because they tend to move in this way – rather than in straight lines. Dan will not ask a horse to do anything that he would not do himself.

6 Dan is aiming at the lightest feel possible to gain a response from the horse. He demonstrates here the physical feel as in the very light contact on this rein. However, it is the mental connection with the horse that he is primarily interested in and he aims for an eighth of an ounce of pressure on the horse's mind to get what he needs. Notice how the horse's ear and eye are locked on to Dan.

7 Ann shows how the focus of the rider is important. By keeping calm and centred she can walk the horse over this pole fence, without changing the rhythm during the approach, over the fence and afterwards.

Thanks to Brookfield Farm Acorn Way, Spondon, Derby, for the use of their facilities for the Dan Franklin photographs.

Natural Horse•Man•Ship

Ex-rodeo rider Pat Parelli believes that everyone can learn to have 'feel for horses' and he has developed his systematic approach to horsemanship as a result of his own life's work with horses. Pat had moved from success in rodeos to training horses when a combination of events occurred in his life. He met Australian horseman Tony Ernst who was also a martial arts expert. As a result of this meeting, Pat learnt about mind-body mastery and inner power. Under the tutelage of Californian horseman Troy Henry, Pat came to understand horse psychology and the art of communicating with a prey animal. The lessons from these horsemen, together with Pat's experience of working with mules, set him on a path to formulate his own way of teaching people. He felt that if people could get enough control over themselves, physically, mentally and emotionally, they could then use horse psychology to communicate their wishes to their horses.

Parelli Natural Horse•Man•Ship (PNH), as developed by Pat and his wife Linda, is now taught worldwide: the aim of the Parellis' educational programme is to raise the standards of horsemanship across the world. The programme teaches people to teach horses – and students develop as individuals because they stretch themselves mentally, emotionally and physically when working through the levels. Ground skills are given just as much prominence as ridden skills as Parelli students aim to become all-round horsemen by being skilled with horses on a line, at liberty, riding freestyle and riding with finesse.

CHANGING YOURSELF

In Pat's system of teaching people to teach horses he lists six keys to success:

• 1 Attitude

As they work through his programme, many people realize that they need to change themselves. Becoming a horseman is a journey, and inevitably there are times when feelings of anger, frustration and despair creep in. By being prepared to change and by developing an attitude whereby they are prepared to make mistakes, to learn from them and their experiences, people make progress. They learn to accept their responsibilities in the partnership deal. As Pat says, 'Be positive, progressive and natural.'

• 2 Knowledge

Pat stresses the importance of learning about everything to do with horses – like understanding their behaviour, how they think and learn, what is important to them, how to communicate with them – instead of just concentrating on riding. He uses a variety of methods to pass on knowledge including instruction, videos, audio tapes and courses.

• 3 Tools

The tools have been designed to aid communication with the horse. They include a rope halter, long ropes and a carrot stick (a stiff orange-coloured stick used as an extension of your arm, not as a whip).

• 4 Techniques

Communication is the key word. Pat says his techniques are there to ensure that communication between horse and handler is very clear. The right attitude and focus from the handler is important and Pat believes that working through his system will enable a person to develop a feel for the horse.

• 5 Time

This has to be invested if both horse and handler are to improve.

• 6 Imagination

The Parelli programme involves lots of tasks to show people how to be more creative with the time they spend with their horses, so that the horses can be stimulated mentally, physically and emotionally.

Natural Horse•Man•Ship

THE SEVEN GAMES

The basis of the whole Parelli programme is the Seven Games. These are based upon how horses, and particularly a mare and foal, interact. Within a short time of giving birth, the mare must teach her foal to go forwards, backwards and sideways so that he is able to keep out of trouble. The mare will use varying levels of pressure, from a light touch to a nip if necessary, but ideally the foal will learn to respond to the very lightest pressure.

By teaching your horse the Seven Games you will increase his confidence and self-esteem, show him how to yield to and from pressure, build his trust in you and show him that he can try whatever you ask without resisting. You will be 'talking' to him in a language he understands and from this you can progress to much higher levels of communication.

PRINCIPLE AND PURPOSE

The first three games are known as the 'Principle' games, and the rest are the 'Purpose' games. Always work through the games in order and make sure you can do one really well before moving on to the next. If you get into trouble, go back a step and re-establish the early work.

STUDY PARELLI

There are 3 levels in Pat's programme aimed at teaching people to understand horses:

• Partnership – Basic skills and safety (level 1)

• Harmony – Intermediate skills and fun (level 2)

• Refinement – Foundation for excellence (level 3)

There are a further 7 levels aimed at training horses and the higher levels of these involve study time with Pat Parelli.

GAME ONE – THE FRIENDLY GAME

This game is based on the fact that the mare licks her foal all over when he is born to help bond with him, to stimulate his body and to reassure him. Its purpose is to establish you as the horse's friend. During the game you touch the horse all over with your hands, then a rope and then the carrot stick. This helps to build trust and desensitizes the horse to contact, helping him to become more confident. The game is also used throughout training to reassure a horse if he gets confused or anxious and also to let him know that he has done the right thing. The objective is for the horse to accept all the games without being scared or confused.

TIPS

- Touch your horse with sensitivity and love, as a mare touches her foal.

- Be considerate to your horse – ask his permission to enter his space.

- If your horse tries to kick you when you touch a sensitive spot, use the carrot stick to help desensitize him. Keep the horse's head slightly turned towards you so that he cannot swing his quarters round to you.

1 The carrot stick is used to accustom a horse to being touched on the hindquarters.

2 This horse is totally relaxed as Ingela swings the carrot stick rhythmically around his head. The objective of the friendly game is for your horse to see you as a friend and not as a threat.

Natural Horse•Man•Ship

GAME TWO – THE PORCUPINE GAME

This teaches a horse to follow a feel and to move away from steady pressure. It acts as preparation for the horse to respond to pressure from the bit or the rider's leg. You apply pressure in four phases, starting with a very light pressure and increasing if the horse does not respond. As soon as the horse responds, release the pressure.

Here Ingela is using fingertip pressure to move her horse's front end. Note her body position as well – she is very positive and clear in her intentions.

The horse is being taught to yield to steady pressure. This is initially applied to the chest, front end and hindquarters so that you can move him in any direction. At first a carrot stick is used to apply the pressure but a horse soon learns to yield to the lightest touch of the handler's fingertips.

TIP
• Use a steady pressure, not a poking motion.

TIP
• Think about your own position. Are you in the right place or will you cause your horse to move in the wrong direction?

Note how the horse is relaxed throughout and is yielding to pressure without resistance. His steps are deliberate and calm.

2: Groundwork in Practice

GAME THREE – THE DRIVING GAME

This is similar to the second game in that the horse learns to move away from pressure but this time it is without the handler touching him. Instead you suggest pressure by the use of body language and by tapping the carrot stick on the ground or along the rope and you drive the horse in all four directions. When he responds to the carrot stick, you progress to using your hands in its place, simply tapping the air in front of the horse to move him.

TIPS
- Just ask for a few steps at first.
- Make obvious use of your body language and your energy so that your horse is very clear about your intentions.

In the driving game, the handler does not touch the horse so she has to make her intentions clear by her body position and her body energy.

Note the slack in the line and how relaxed the horse is. He is paying attention and responding to Ingela's positive intention, calmly moving his hindquarters over.

Games Four to Seven are the Purpose Games. They are based on combining the skills learnt in Games One to Three, and mean you can start to be more productive with your horse.

GAME FOUR – THE YO-YO GAME

This teaches the horse to go backwards and come forwards easily, remaining straight and balanced. In effect, Game Four is a combination of Games Two and Three. The four phases of pressure can be used but the ultimate aim is to bring your horse towards you with just a signal from your hand, and without a rope being used. Concentrate on getting the forward and back motion first. Once you have this you can start to think about the horse's straightness.

Ingela uses a very light signal to ask her horse to back up and then come forward to her. The ultimate aim is to be able to do this without a rope, just using your fingers to motion your horse towards you.

TIPS

- If you hit problems, reassess how well your horse does Games Two and Three. Go back and practise these games before trying the Yo-Yo Game again.

- Start off slowly. Once your horse is really good you can get creative, such as playing the Yo-Yo Game on a hill or over a pole.

GAME FIVE – THE CIRCLING GAME

One of the purposes of this game is to help the horse understand two of his responsibilities – that he does not change gait or direction until he is asked. Basically, the game consists of the horse being sent out on to a circle, travelling around the handler. You use body language to send the horse out on to the circle, to maintain direction and travel on the circle and to bring the horse back – whereby you ask him to turn in and face you. The game teaches the horse to look for you and come to you, especially if he is confused. As you progress through the Parelli levels, you will work your horse at liberty with lots of other horses around and these games provide the basis for your later work.

TIPS

- Start off in walk and build up to trot as you become more proficient. Do not ask your horse to canter as the circle is too small.
- This game is not lungeing. Do not bore your horse by asking him to do too many circles. Four good laps is your objective.

Ingela's horse has learnt that it is his responsibility to stay in the gait requested and move in the direction requested until he is asked to do otherwise. While he is doing this Ingela can be relaxed in the middle of the circle.

GAME SIX – THE SIDEWAYS GAME

This game teaches a horse that he can go left and right equally and with ease. Start off by having your horse facing a fence so that his forward movement is blocked, then use rhythmic pressure at his head and hindquarters to move him sideways. Ultimately, the game is played without the assistance of a fence line.

TIPS

- Start off in walk and get this really established before you try the game at a trot.
- All horses will find one direction more easy than the other. Work equally on your horse's difficult side until he finds going either way easy.
- Make sure you walk in a positive and purposeful manner.

When you first learn the sideways game, you play it along a fence line, so that it is easier for you to move your horse sideways. Here Ingela demonstrates how the game can be developed as she moves her horse sideways in either direction in an open space.

Natural Horse•Man•Ship

2: Groundwork in Practice

GAME SEVEN – THE SQUEEZE GAME

In this game, you ask your horse to go between you and an object such as a fence. It is great preparation for life in the human world where a horse will face all sorts of situations that go against his instincts – being loaded, for instance, because being confined in this way prevents him from fleeing from danger. As well as helping your horse to overcome his phobias, the game assists with tasks such as crossing streams and jumping.

IN CONCLUSION...

This foundation work is invaluable. Once you have mastered these games, you may find that some difficulties you had with your horse have disappeared. For instance, the Friendly Game helps overcome problems such as being irritable to groom or difficult to bridle or clip, while lateral work is much easier under saddle once your horse can do it easily in-hand.

Through these games you learn how to think like a horse so that you can present things to him in a way that he will understand, and your horse learns that you are a reliable leader. As a result your relationship will improve as both of you learn to appreciate each other.

TIPS
- Do not make the space through which he has to pass too narrow at first. You can gradually decrease the size down – say to 1m (3ft) wide – as his confidence grows.
- Work in walk initially. Once your horse is happy going both ways in walk, you can move on to doing the exercise in trot.

This horse is happy to go through a small gap – the Squeeze Game helps to prepare horses for loading and with other phobias. This game can be used to help horses with their jumping as through the game they learn to go forwards, calmly and confidently.

CASE STUDY: An active retirement – putting natural horsemanship into practice

Applejack had always been in regular work, which included going to riding club competitions, pleasure rides and the occasional day's hunting. However, intermittent lameness kept striking the 19-year-old horse and eventually the cause was found to be degenerative disease in one knee.

Retirement followed but it soon became evident that Applejack missed his work. So Will, his owner, decided to keep the old horse's mind stimulated by using some of the Parelli Natural Horsemanship games. Will had seen some Parelli videos and thought there was scope to keep Applejack entertained while helping to maintain his suppleness, co-ordination and balance.

The old horse was a quick learner and seemed to enjoy his sessions in the arena. Will also enjoyed spending time with his horse and felt that the bond between them was as strong as ever.

Four years on and Applejack is enjoying his retirement which is punctuated by fun sessions in the arena playing the Parelli Games. The horse is free in his movement, relatively supple and mentally is very bright and playful.

Will has also used some of the principles learnt via Parelli to improve the mobility of his second horse. This new horse found it difficult to execute turns on the haunches and forehand, but found it much easier once Will used the Porcupine Game to get him moving around freely.

Think Equus

2: Groundwork in Practice

Think Equus is Michael Peace's way of working with horses – a non-confrontational approach that promotes mutual respect and a true partnership that benefits both horse and rider. Horse and rider have their responsibilities within the partnership and each has to be responsible for their own actions, working with each other second by second and adjusting to the situation accordingly. Neither partner is dominant, although the rider may have to control the situations they experience in order to ensure the safety of both.

Michael often meets 'problem' horses that very soon change their attitude when they realize that he is there to help them. This change in attitude is achieved because Michael does not necessarily react in the way the horses have come to expect. For instance, the horse pictured here is normally aggressive towards people who approach him in his stable (top left). He may be like this for various reasons, perhaps he is territorial about his stable or food, or at some point in his life he may have been abused in his stable and feels that his best defence is to be on the attack.

As you can see, Michael does not respond by being aggressive in return. He quietly stands his ground – you can see that his body language is soft but he is very aware of the horse at all times. This is not how people normally react to this horse and within seconds he has recognized this and starts to show an interest in Michael.

As the horse becomes more interested and less aggressive, Michael rewards him with a rub on the head. Within a few minutes Michael goes into the horse's stable. Initially, the horse moves away when Michael enters and flattens his ears again. Michael feels that this aggressive behaviour is because the horse prefers to be left alone, so he does not pursue the horse but waits quietly near the door. With his interest aroused, the horse turns to Michael and approaches him. Michael rubs him on the head as a reward and the two are soon friends. The horse's attitude has changed because he realizes there is neither the need nor any benefit in being aggressive with Michael.

Learning to understand and think like a horse is an important element of Think Equus. By appreciating how a horse lives with his peers, how he sees the world, why he reacts as he does and what motivates him, we can pinpoint why problems are happening and work out how to address the root cause, rather than just deal with the symptoms.

Think Equus

THE KEY ELEMENTS

Two major elements of Think Equus are exercises devised with the aim of gaining your horse's respect and his attention, and to achieve a 50/50 partnership with your horse.

RESPECT AND ATTENTION

This exercise to achieve respect and attention is basically a leading exercise with plenty of changes of direction and pace. The work is done in a normal headcollar but with a longer than average rope.

Do this exercise in an environment where your horse will not be easily distracted – you want to set up the situation to encourage success. You can start off in your horse's stable – ask him to take a step towards you by taking up the slack in the rope. Reward him with a rub on the head when he does. Then step to the other side and ask your horse to come towards you again, rewarding him when he does. It will not take long for him to realize that coming towards you results in him feeling good.

Once this is working well in a stable, transfer to a round pen or an arena. Position yourself out in front of the horse and have plenty of slack in the rope. Walk off confidently and your horse should follow – if he doesn't he will get a bump from the rope when the slack disappears. Make lots of changes of direction as you want your horse to have to concentrate on you and your next move. Every time you stop, your horse should stop too. If he walks past you or stops too close to you, then you have to back him up. The horse has to learn to respect your personal space, just as he would respect the space of other horses in a herd.

1 This student on a Think Equus course has problems with her horse moving while she is trying to mount. The first step to solving the problem is doing the leading work to get his respect and attention. As the student stops walking, it becomes clear that her horse is not paying her sufficient attention...

3 Therefore the student backs up the horse. Rather than pushing him away it would have been better to have wiggled the rope at him, making him responsible for moving back. Always be clear and definite in your instructions.

4 Now that she has the horse correctly positioned she rewards him and lets him stand there for a short while. Horses soon learn to take responsibility for their actions.

2 ... he simply walks on past her. To teach her horse that stopping on time is his side of the deal, the student has to show him what to do. It's important to stays emotionally detached from the situation – there's no point in getting cross with him for not stopping. Adopting a more business-like approach gets you in the right frame of mind. You and the horse are there because succeeding in getting this job done will make life better for both of you.

Think Equus

2: Groundwork in Practice

THE 50/50 PARTNERSHIP

Achieving a 50/50 partnership with a horse is not easy, but followers of Think Equus will always be striving for it. Much of the horse world operates on the basis that the human half of a partnership has at least 51 per cent of the power, however Michael believes that equal shares result in a much better whole as both parties are then 100 per cent committed to the success of the partnership.

To achieve and then maintain the 50/50 balance, both parties must make constant minute changes to the relationship – it's a case of both horse and handler meeting each other halfway. Horses know all about co-operation as they live in a society where co-operation is vital for happy communal living.

If you are being reasonable and clear about what you expect your horse to do then he should make an effort and co-operate. If he cannot be bothered you are entitled to get after him. How you 'get after your horse' is crucial. There is absolutely no place in Think Equus for the abuse of a horse. When Michael says 'get after' a horse he means that he makes life a tad uncomfortable. The point is well illustrated here (right), with Michael dealing with a difficult loader.

1 This horse has a 90/10 balance over his owner. He barges out of the stable …

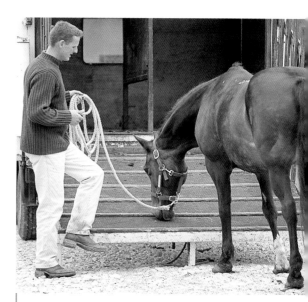

1 Here, Michael is dealing with a difficult loader. If the horse is paying attention and trying to overcome his fears then Michael will leave him alone and give him time to work out what needs to be done.

2 However, if the horse is not trying and is allowing himself to be distracted or is just planting himself, then Michael will 'hassle' him. This can take the form of waving a coiled-up rope beside him or using a rope around the quarters to get the hind legs moving again. The second the horse starts to try again, Michael removes the hassle factor.

2 …and drags her all the way to the field. The owner has allowed him to use his physical strength against her.

THE MIDDLE GROUND

- Unfortunately, many horses receive harsh treatment – perhaps being beaten with whips, having their sides kicked by spurs, or being forced into a trailer. The person handing out the treatment has allowed frustration or anger to get the better of them and has taken out their own inadequacies on the horse. Sad as this is, it's made even worse by the fact that the horse probably hasn't got the faintest idea why he's been beaten.

- Michael believes that horses have an area of tolerance, which he calls the middle ground, within which they will allow you to make a mistake without taking advantage of you or resenting you. The more 'innocent' the horse, the larger the middle ground. For example, an unspoilt youngster who has never been mistreated and always handled fairly will have a large area of middle ground or tolerance, while a horse that has been abused will have very little tolerance left – his middle ground might only be a fine line. This is why problem horses need a greater understanding and careful handling by an experienced trainer such as Michael.

- People who abuse horses are working way outside the middle ground – and their behaviour means that the horse has no choice but to fight them or be submissive to them. In the latter cases, the horses are often totally switched off as that is the only way they can deal with life. Whatever has caused the fight will, therefore, remain a problem. The classic example of this is the horse that has been forced to load. He will usually put up a fight every time attempts are made to load him, and each time the force needed to get him into the trailer will be increased. However, if a horse has been allowed to make a conscious decision to walk into a trailer he will be happy to do so every time.

Case Study: A Lack of Trust

2: Groundwork in Practice

This horse's new owner is keen to help him but she has a problem, she often cannot get near him and when she does, he is aggressive towards her. The problem is compounded by the fact that the horse's companion has been taken away from him. Michael visits the pair and explains that overcoming the problem will take time. His purpose on this first visit is to show the owner how to start changing her horse's attitude so that she can catch him.

1 This horse's anxiety at being separated from his friend is evident by the poached ground beside the fence – the horse clearly spends a lot of time walking and trotting along this line. As Michael enters the field, the horse turns to look but does not move from the fence.

2 Michael approaches the horse and even though his body language is passive the horse starts to behave aggressively.

TIPS

- Learn all you can about horse psychology – you have to understand life from the horse's viewpoint in order to train him humanely and effectively.

- Set yourself up for success by making it easy for your horse to do the right thing.

- Think about the consequences of your actions before you act. Change or adjust your plan accordingly.

- Think carefully about the level of the lesson you are presenting to your horse. Is it too much for him to take in? Or are you likely to bore him? Each horse has his own learning pace – you must be aware of this so you can keep him stimulated but not overfaced or bored.

- Remember, horses learn bad practices just as easily as good ones!

- Let your horse know that you are there to help him. Be consistent, clear and fair.

3 Instead of backing off at this behaviour, Michael continues to move around the horse, describing large arcs around him and increasing the horse's awareness and tolerance of him.

4 Michael succeeds in getting the horse's attention and causing a small shift in his attitude. As the horse's interest is aroused, Michael is able to draw him away from the fence line and towards him. Michael wants to show the horse that the presence of a human can be enjoyable.

5 The horse follows Michael in a non-aggressive manner. As Michael wants to make contact with him, he returns to the fence where the horse spends his time.

6 At the fence, Michael halts and waits for the horse to approach him. His body language is passive – note the soft rounded shoulders – but he is aware of where the horse is.

7 The horse is now very interested – note his ears. Michael stays calm and does not try to make contact with the horse too soon. Both horse and Michael are observing each other second by second.

8 The horse checks out Michael. The fact that he has turned from aggressive to interested in such a short time shows that he is willing to change his behaviour. Being on the alert all the time is wearing for him and he takes the opportunity to find an easier way to live.

9 As Michael raises his head and makes a slight adjustment to his body, the horse reacts instinctively – note the ears, tail and the body tension. But, he does not react as he normally does by actually being aggressive, nor does he move away.

10 The horse has tried hard to work in a partnership and Michael lets him know that he has done the right thing by giving him a rub on the head, the first contact the horse has had for some time. This is only the beginning for this horse but by using the Think Equus principles Michael has made huge progress in a very short time.

Positive Horse Magic

2: Groundwork in Practice

Positive Horse Magic is a system of training horses developed by Heather and Ross Simpson, drawing upon their knowledge, understanding and experience of horse psychology and using positive reinforcement.

The idea of positive reinforcement is well known and extensively used in training dogs and dolphins, but is relatively new in the horse world. It is based upon a system of rewards that are important to the animal, such as food, playing games or giving your attention. By rewarding your horse for good behaviour you are actively encouraging him to repeat his good experience. Heather and Ross find that through positive reinforcement horses become more motivated and enthusiastic about their training sessions.

Traditionally, much of the training of horses has revolved around negative reinforcement. For example, a horse being loaded into the trailer, has to choose the lesser of two evils, that is either he goes into the trailer, or he faces being whacked with a brush. But loading can also be taught through positive reinforcement, which will reward him for all his attempts to do what he is asked.

From the horse's point of view, positive reinforcement is a pleasant experience while at best, negative reinforcement results in a 'grin and bear it' attitude. Horses play throughout their lives if all their other needs (such as feeling safe, being able to feed and rest, and being with friends) are met. A horse's innate play patterns can be used to assist with their training.

This sequence illustrates how a form of positive reinforcement, known as clicker training, has motivated and enthused Ross's horse, Bjorn.

Clicker training involves a gadget, called a clicker, that makes a clicking noise. The trainer presses the clicker so that the horse hears the click at the very instant that his good behaviour occurs. The click, which is also paired with a treat, such as a food reward, marks the behaviour that you want from the horse. Once the horse associates a reward, such as food, with the sound of the clicker, the food can be replaced by a word – good, for example. The next step is to phase out the clicker so that the word alone acts as a marker for the behaviour and a reward.

Bjorn is doing what most horses love, he's grazing at liberty in a large field. However, he has become so confident and enthusiastic about his work that he happily stops grazing and accepts Ross's invitation to play.

Positive Horse Magic

These photographs show the initial stages of clicker training. The trainer can build on this foundation work to teach the horse the various skills needed to survive in the domesticated world, for instance how to load into a trailer.

TIPS
- If you help your horse to win through enabling him to have lots of small successes and rewarding him for his efforts, he'll learn quicker.
- Research has shown that our short-term memory has a number of slots that we can fill with information – there are usually between seven and nine slots. If you give your horse too much information, he won't have enough slots in his memory to cope and the learning process will be slowed down.

1 Ross has the clicker in his left hand ready to click the instant the required behaviour is performed, and a small amount of food (to be given as a reward) in his right hand. Timing is vital as the horse has to associate his behaviour with a click and treat.

② The concept of being rewarded for an action is introduced by Ross holding a cone in front of Bjorn, close to his nose. When Bjorn touches the cone, he is rewarded with a click and a treat.

③ Once the horse will touch the cone when it is held in front and to the side of him, it's time to teach him to touch the cone on the ground. This behaviour can then be used to encourage a horse to take steps into a trailer, to go past strange objects and so on.

④ Touching large objects, such as giant footballs, can also lead to games, building a horse's confidence and self-esteem. A lack of confidence often shows itself as a behavioural problem, which this form of positive reinforcement training can help overcome.

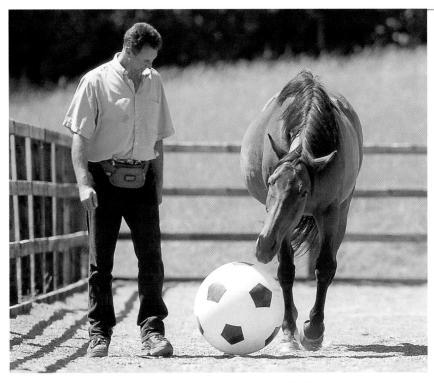

TTEAM

All TTEAM work aims to help a horse's balance, co-ordination and body awareness, to ensure that mentally, physically and emotionally, the horse is the best he can be. It is carried out slowly so that he has time to understand what is required of him. Working through a problem slowly also gives a horse time to learn properly. If everything is rushed, there is an element of fear or anxiety, which hampers the learning process. To achieve their aims, TTEAM practitioners focus on leading exercises and obstacles, such as wooden platforms, various arrangements of poles and working with plastic sheets.

TTEAM LEADING POSITIONS

TTEAM has a variety of leading positions to help the horse according to its specific problems. For example, horses that barge often do so because they have poor balance and do not know where their boundaries are. As they encourage lightening of the forehand and engagement of the hindquarters, the leading positions enable a horse to carry himself in a more effective way, and they enable the handler to control the horse's head, and in turn, his body. They are non-habitual, so the horse is encouraged to think and learn in a new way.

SARAH FISHER

After training as a practitioner of massage and aromatherapy for people, Sarah Fisher, who is featured here, became the highest qualified TTOUCH and TTEAM Practitioner in Britain after training with Linda Tellington-Jones and Robyn Hood in the USA.

1 This is a basic leading position and the handler has chosen to lead from the offside. Horses are normally handled from the nearside, which means that all their muscles and their nervous system have developed for this. As a result, the right side of the horse is often stiff. By switching to the offside for leading, the handler is helping to redress this.

2 Using the wand (see Tips, above right) to show the horse the way forward. The wand is used to help to focus a horse, and it can often calm a nervous horse. It is also used in various ways to move the horse, ask him to stop, or to bring his attention to something.

3 Some horses have very little awareness of the extremities of their bodies. Here, stroking the wand down the horse's legs helps to heighten his awareness and 'ground' him.

TIPS

- Two of the main tools used in TTEAM are the wand and the chain lead line.

- The chain lead line is used to give very light signals to the horse. A much more precise signal can be given with a chain than with a rope, which is useful when dealing with stronger horses. The chain lead line should never be used in an abusive way; horses are never tied up with chain lead lines. Sensitive or young horses may prefer the TTEAM zephyr lead, which has soft rope.

- Along with the lead line, the wand and the voice are also used to give clear signals to the horse.

- Staying out in front and to the side of the horse means that he can see you more easily, helping him to understand and respond to your instructions.

- When a horse is halted, the wand is used to tap on the chest or shoulder, so encouraging him to take his weight back and halt in better balance.

4 The wand is a useful tool for attracting a horse's attention or asking him to stay out of your space. It can be used to safely achieve both these objectives.

TTEAM

CONFIDENCE BUILDERS

Teaching a horse to step willingly onto a strange surface, such as the wooden bridge (below) and the seesaw (right), is good preparation for hazards that might be met out hacking, such as wooden bridges and stream crossings, and for learning to step up the ramp into a trailer or lorry without anxiety.

1 Sarah has worked on building up trust in this horse before she asks him to walk onto this strange surface. The rail can be used to teach a horse to go through narrow spaces or it can be hung with sheets of plastic or other items that might initially concern a horse. Showing a horse how to overcome his fears builds his self-confidence and self-esteem.

2 Sarah uses the wand to slow down the horse and assist his balance. The horse's brain is dealing with the sensation and sound of the change of surface. She gives him time to get used to it. This experience will help when it comes to loading him.

3 Once again she uses the wand to focus the horse's attention before she asks him to step off the platform. The speed of this step has to be controlled, but other work on the ground will have taught him to move one foot at a time.

4 She moves the wand away from the horse to signal to him that he can move forward.

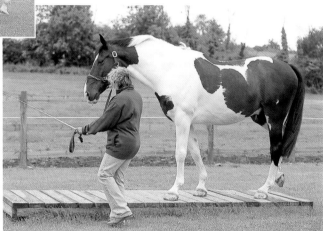

THE SEESAW

Once the horse is happy with stepping on and off the basic platform, halting on it and moving as requested, he can progress to the seesaw, a more challenging exercise.

1 This platform pivots in the middle like a seesaw. Learning to walk calmly over it while it is in motion is good practice for loading and is also valuable for horses that freeze inside the trailer and are difficult to unload.

2 Once he has stepped on, Sarah halts the horse and draws his attention to his legs and feet by stroking the wand down his legs and tapping it on his feet.

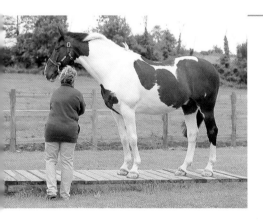

3 Directed by Sarah, the horse continues to walk along the seesaw, taking one step at a time. She steadies him just before the pivot point and makes him aware of his feet again, then asks him to walk on moving one foot at a time.

4 The horse reaches the other side of the seesaw, without being worried by the seesaw motion. Having done the earlier work such as moving one foot at a time on request, it usually takes a couple of 20-minute sessions to achieve this.

TIPS
- Build a horse's self-confidence with obstacles like these.
- Teach your horse to wait for signals from his handler.
- These exercises increase your horse's awareness of his own body and he will learn to think about what he is doing.

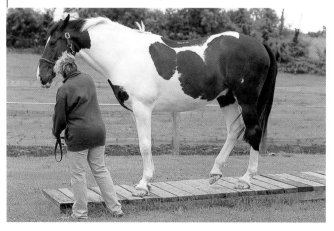

TTEAM

CO-ORDINATION IMPROVERS

2: Groundwork in Practice

Working with arrangements of poles helps horses improve their co-ordination, balance, obedience, self-control and suppleness. From the handler's point of view, this work increases their awareness of the horse's movement and areas of difficulty while improving their own dexterity in leading the horse and helping him to master the obstacle.

THE LABYRINTH AND THE STAR

The labyrinth (here and pages 98–9) can be used for horses of all ages. It can help young horses that have not yet been started to gain a better awareness of where to place their feet and how to balance, and it can help settle a lively horse before more serious ridden work begins. The star (pages 100–101) can increase confidence, relax nervous horses and assist with flexion, co-ordination and balance.

1 Use 4m (12ft) poles to build the labyrinth as shown. Space the poles 1.2m (4ft) apart but increase this distance if your horse has trouble negotiating the turns.

2 Start leading your horse through the poles, beginning with a bend on his most comfortable rein. The labyrinth teaches a horse to work from behind, cross his legs behind and to bring his legs forward.

3 Move slowly. Although to us it is clear what is required, a horse needs time to organize himself and work out what is needed. Doing this exercise will indicate any problems you can expect to experience when the horse is under saddle. For example, your horse might have difficulty in turning one way or he might be out of balance.

4 Continue moving slowly to allow the horse to learn – rushing will not teach him anything. If he rushes to get through this indicates that he is suffering from a lack of balance. Slow him down and make sure you halt before each turn to give him time to collect himself and move the correct legs.

5 Ensure you give him enough room to manoeuvre – you can step into another section of the labyrinth if necessary. Observe how your horse negotiates the turn. You should see an improvement in how he uses himself as you work through the exercise.

2: Groundwork in Practice

CO-ORDINATION IMPROVERS

THE LABYRINTH (continued)

6 Try halting around the turn as this is beneficial for your horse's balance. To relax him as you work, stroke down his front legs with the wand. This also gives him a different focus if something else has attracted his attention.

7 To help your horse around the turn if he seems to be falling inward or forward, raise his head.

8 As you come off a turn, use the wand on the offside shoulder (inset) to make him more aware and to prevent his quarters from swinging around. Work through the labyrinth on both reins and make sure you give your horse plenty of praise for his efforts. Avoid the temptation to go on repeating the exercise until he starts to make mistakes. It is better to stop early, on a good note, give him a break and let him think about it.

9 An alternative use of the labyrinth is to walk across it, letting your horse step over the poles.

10 If he finds this difficult, help him by tapping the poles with the wand, drawing attention to them and focusing his thoughts.

2: Groundwork in Practice

CO-ORDINATION IMPROVERS

THE STAR

1 To practise the star, lay the poles on the ground as shown, about 1.2m (4ft) apart at the open end. When you begin, start where they are widest apart and once he has gained confidence, move in to where the distances between the poles are smaller. To negotiate these poles your horse has to improve his co-ordination, and his flexibility will be enhanced with time. If a horse is really stiff, start working over only two or three poles.

2 To increase the difficulty of the exercise raise the poles slightly. This helps to improve the flexion through the horse's barrel so it's good for horses that find lateral work difficult. Start off at the outer edge again. Make sure you are in advance of the horse so that he has room to see what he has to do and can adjust his balance. Ring the changes – raise alternate ends or the poles in the middle – so your horse always has to think.

3 Move closer in and repeat the exercise. You can see how much more the horse has to use his joints. Work from both directions and lead him from both sides.

4 This is hard work for the handler, too! Your horse may well mimic you if you exaggerate stepping over the poles. Keep your horse on a loose lead line and do not pull him around the star.

TIPS

- Most horses are not taught how to use their bodies – TTEAM leading positions and groundwork exercises help the horse to be aware of his body and make him use it more effectively. Horses that are physically out of balance are often mentally and emotionally out of balance as well. If your horse is out of balance, these exercises will soon reveal it.

- Observe how your horse moves around the turns in a labyrinth. With a little practice he should step around easily rather than shuffle.

- Use stepping over poles to help nervous horses gain confidence and relax tense horses.

- Use these exercises to increase sure-footedness in horses that stumble and make those that have trouble bending more supple.

- The labyrinth and star exercises are good for horses that are worried by travelling as they teach them to co-ordinate each limb and to move with precision.

- This polework stimulates the mind and is good for horses that have restricted turnout during winter. It is also useful for settling horses that are very fresh when they first come out for work.

- Working through the star arrangement helps neck flexion. It also indicates whether a horse is likely to hang to one side under saddle – a horse will fall out through the shoulder if he is not working from behind.

- Challenge your horse by making the poles in the star uneven heights.

- Spooky horses are often out of balance and tight in their neck – work over the raised poles brings up their wither and shoulder and allows the neck to lengthen.

- You will find that working your horse from both sides through the labyrinth improves your own suppleness so you become less one-sided.

TTEAM

CHEST-LINE DRIVING

Chest-line driving is the TTEAM alternative to long-reining. It is used to start all young horses and also as a remedial tool for older horses with schooling issues such as rushing at fences, falling through the shoulders or if the horse is nervous of things that are behind him.

2 The pony is introduced to the feel of the line along his back and flank by winding the line around the wand and then stroking him with the wand and line.

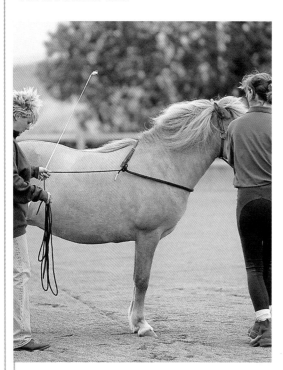

1 A balancing rein is put around the horse's neck and a chest line is attached to one side of the balancing rein.

3 A handler walks at the pony's head while the driver, Sarah, walks behind. The pony has to be given time to become accustomed to someone in front and behind him and, at first, Sarah ensures the rein does not touch him. Both handlers observe his reactions at all times.

4 Gradually the pony is introduced to the feel of the line being in contact with his side.

5 The second line is now attached on the other side. Every new experience is introduced gradually, building the pony's confidence.

6 As soon as the pony is happy being driven, work can start. Chest-line driving can be used with TTEAM obstacles and poles.

Case Study: Scared of Jumping

COMBINING GROUNDWORK TECHNIQUES

Sam's jumping ability meant that as a young horse he was pushed to keep achieving more. He was doing his best to clear the fences but was jumping 'with his eyes closed' as Michael Peace would say. This means that he was jumping as quickly as he could, simply to get the job done, rather than going round in a relaxed happy manner. So worried was Sam that his approaches to fences became faster and faster. Eventually he tipped up, hurting both himself and his rider. As a result he was sold on a couple of times before eventually finding an owner who recognized that Sam rushed his fences because of fear and also pain (he had not received any treatment after his fall and had been compensating ever since).

Sam's new owner decided to forget about jumping and concentrate on getting him physically and emotionally well again. She could see from his muscular development that he had problems, so she called in an Equine Muscle Release Therapist. In turn this therapist suggested that a McTimoney chiropractor was also needed as Sam's pelvis was rotated and he had some vertebral misalignments in his neck and back as a result of upending himself.

As a matter of course, Sam's teeth and saddle were also checked. His teeth had some nasty hooks on the left-hand side, which would have been causing him considerable pain. After Sam's EMRT treatments, he altered shape physically and his saddle had to be changed for a wider one.

With the help of both therapists Sam's condition improved and he became pain free, which had an effect not only on how he moved but also on his temperament. Freed from continual discomfort, he became a much happier horse.

Then the work started on re-educating him. In the past, Sam had been hunted hard, as he could jump big fences and had plenty of stamina. However, his flatwork was pretty basic so he was taken right back to the start. Initially, when he was lunged, Sam acted as if he was on a 'wall of death' circuit, shooting round and round the school at breakneck speed and with a complete lack of balance. To calm him and slow him down he was introduced to in-hand work and to TTEAM polework, which also made him think.

Another benefit of these ground exercises was that Sam became more aware of his body. Sam's suppleness, balance and co-ordination improved and when he was ridden again there was a marked difference in his performance under saddle. He was much calmer and more accepting of the rider's aids.

Because Sam had progressed so well, his owner introduced a small fence. On the first couple of attempts Sam was very calm and obediently trotted towards and over the fence without rushing. Then he suddenly reverted to his old ways and flew towards the fence. It is clear from this that Sam's re-education still has some way to go. His owner believes she tried to re-introduce jumping too soon and is now going back a few steps to consolidate her work to date. She is thinking that she will try jumping Sam loose or on a long-line Parelli-style, to help him realize that it is nothing to be worried about.

1 Sam's muscular problems were addressed by the author, Lesley Bayley, who is also an Equine Muscle Release Therapy practitioner.

2 TTEAM bodywork and groundwork exercises helped Sam become aware of his body and has improved his suppleness and co-ordination.

3 Jumping on line and at liberty, Parelli-style, is being considered for Sam, in order to re-build his confidence.

Lungeing

THE GREAT DEBATE

Lungeing is a subject that has both advocates and detractors.

THOSE IN FAVOUR

Those in favour use lungeing for various reasons, including:

- as a means of providing exercise
- as part of starting a young horse
- for improvement of a horse's balance, self carriage and paces
- for the training and retraining of older horses
- for development of a horse's muscles without the added strain of a rider
- to teach a horse to go forward in balance

THOSE AGAINST

Those against say that lungeing:

- can put too much strain on a horse's joints
- can, if done badly, do more harm than good to the horse's balance, co-ordination and muscular development
- can confuse the horse

They argue that when being lunged the horse is expected to move *forwards* from pressure on one side, but that when we ride or do other types of groundwork we want him to go *sideways* from pressure on one side, when we ask him to move over in a stable, for example.

Whether or not to lunge is an individual choice. The important point is that any skill has to be learnt and then applied properly for the horse to benefit. It is helpful to be able to lunge your horse, as you may have to do so occasionally; for example, a vet may ask to see your horse lunged to help with an examination.

TIPS

- If you have never lunged before, arrange to have lessons with a qualified instructor, preferably using a horse that has experienced lungeing so that you can concentrate on your technique.

- Practise handling the lunge rein and whip. Learn how to pay out and take in the rein smoothly, without getting into a muddle. Practise flicking the whip against a target before you go near a horse! The lunge whip should be regarded as the equivalent of your legs when riding. Just as a horse will switch off if the rider's legs are constantly nagging away, so he will become fed up if the whip is used constantly and unfairly.

- Just as in riding, always include warm up, work and then cool down sessions.

- Assess your horse by lungeing him in a cavesson – look at how he moves, whether his gaits are rhythmical and whether he accepts the bit. Ask yourself questions such as: Is he tracking up? Does he look stiff in his back or joints? Is he losing his quarters or falling in or out with his shoulders? Is he taking even steps? Does he move better without his saddle? Is he rushing along? Does he look balanced? This gives you an idea of the points you can work on in lungeing sessions.

Lungeing

The selection and use of lungeing equipment causes much debate, with various schools of thought. Some of the options are shown here but the best way to decide what to do with your horse is to seek help from someone who is knowledgeable and whom you trust. Before you allow anyone to do anything with your horse, watch them at work, so you can gauge whether their approach to handling horses is compatible with your own.

Whether or not to lunge off the bit is a particular area of discussion. There are trainers who like to start lungeing youngsters off the side ring of the headcollar or lungeing cavesson. As the horse becomes more experienced, some trainers like to lunge off the bit rather than a cavesson because it simulates the rider's rein aids and the horse is already accustomed to instructions via the rein and bit so there is no reason to change in order to lunge the horse. Whatever your opinion, do not consider lungeing off the bit until you have gained considerable experience.

WHERE TO LUNGE

Ideally, the lungeing area should be in an arena with a good surface. A sectioned-off corner of your field can be used, provided the going is good, not hard or muddy.

TIP

• If you use a lunge cavesson, make sure you fit it snugly so that the cheek straps are not pulled over your horse's eyes.

1 With a quiet horse the rein can be attached straight onto the inside bit ring. With an exuberant horse, a useful way to fit the lunge rein is to feed it through the inside bit ring over the horse's head and down to the outside bit ring, where it is attached (above). This makes the lunge rein act as an overhead check. This method of attachment is also helpful when lungeing the horse on the rein on which he finds it difficult to take a contact with the bit. It will work very well if the horse is well-balanced and does not lean on the rein. However, it must be used carefully. If the handler is heavy-handed then this arrangement will put undue pressure on the horse.

ALTERNATIVE WAYS OF FITTING THE LUNGE REIN

• For young horses the lunge rein can be attached through the bit ring and the noseband in order to secure it.

TIP

• If you lunge your horse in a saddle ensure that the stirrup irons are secured. Wrap the stirrup leather around the iron and then pass the end of the leather through the stirrup leather keeper. You do not want the irons to drop and swing against the horse's side (especially if it is a young horse that has not yet been accustomed to items swinging against his sides).

2 Rollers or saddles (see Tip, left) can be used when lungeing. Here, the side reins are fitted ready for use once the horse has loosened up. Do not keep a horse standing around in side reins for long periods and always detach them when moving him from stable to arena. This horse is wearing protective leg gear. Boots are more suitable than bandages, however, as the latter may become undone and get caught around the legs or flap around, possibly worrying the horse.

3 Before lungeing in side reins, check them for the correct fit: when the horse is standing in a relaxed position, the rein should reach to the junction between the head and neck. Alternatively, ensure the side rein reaches the jawline of an advanced horse and to the bit ring of a youngster. It is better to start off with looser side reins and adjust them if necessary, especially if the horse has not worked in them before. Fitting them too tightly could result in him becoming upset and throwing himself around.

Lungeing

2: Groundwork in Practice

If your idea of lungeing is the horse whizzing around at the end of a line with the handler struggling to hold on, then you have seen only poor lungeing practice. In such cases, the horse is quite likely to injure himself and his balance, self-confidence and self-carriage are all likely to suffer.

When lungeing there should be slack in the line, showing that the horse is not leaning on the lunge rein and using the handler and rein as a prop.

1 To get into a good position to lunge a horse and deal with any problems, think of a triangle – the horse is the base, the rein is one side, the lunge whip is another side and you are the apex.

2 By forming the apex of a triangle, you can move to either side to drive your horse forward or to slow down the movement. Here Rowan moves to her right – the horse's hindquarters – to ask him to move forward. Keep the triangle in mind – if you move too far forward your horse may turn into the circle.

3 Always be aware of your body position and what you are doing with the lunge whip. Here, the horse is halted and Rowan moves towards him keeping the whip behind her in a passive position.

4 From halt, move a little way towards the horse's hindquarters to be ready to send him forward if he does not respond to the vocal command to walk on.

TIPS

- Use plenty of transitions, just as you would when riding, to improve your horse's suppleness from poll to tail. Work on direct as well as progressive transitions. Ask for downward transitions with a downward inflection of your voice and for upward transitions with an upward and business-like inflection.

- Work on a large circle and on both reins: the horse's inside hind leg has to work harder than the outside one so it is important that you work equally on both reins.

- If your horse is quite lazy on the lunge, walk a circle quite close to him so that you can motivate him.

5 Lungeing gives you the opportunity to see how your horse moves. This horse is being lazy in trot and he is not tracking up. Look at the poor V-shape being made by his legs and compare this to photograph 6, overleaf.

Lungeing

2: Groundwork in Practice

6 To achieve more impulsion, move behind the horse to send him on more and flick the whip towards his hindquarters. Here you can see a much clearer V-shape with Rowan creating more impulsion. Use the lunge rein as you would use a normal rein. For example, half halts can be used to lighten the forehand and contain the energy.

7 Make sure you retain only a light contact on the rein ensuring that the horse carries himself, rather than leaning on you. This horse is staying upright and showing good balance – unbalanced horses tend to 'motorbike' around a circle – he is also straight as his hindfeet are following in the tracks of his forefeet.

8 Make sure your horse is as balanced in trot as possible and carrying himself well before asking for canter. As this horse is used to lunge work he can undertake canter transitions and work in canter without having to rely on the rein.

TIP

- Exercises used under saddle can also be used on the lunge. For instance, use upward and downward transitions, spiral in and out of circles, and move from working to medium paces and back again.

9 However, beware of letting any horse 'motor on' as this results in a loss of balance, which can lead to tripping and possible injury.

10 Allow time for your horse to warm up before lungeing, and cool down afterwards. Always do a few circuits on both reins before attaching any side reins. This horse is lowering his head and moving forward with impulsion, yet in a relaxed way, during his cool down.

Lungeing

LUNGEING EXERCISES

Working over poles and jumps encourages a horse to use himself and to flex his joints, while improving his co-ordination, balance and rhythm. On the lunge, the horse can learn to adjust his balance without the added burden of a rider.

1 Set out the poles on a curve allowing a distance you think is suitable for your horse's stride (about 1.3–1.5m [54–60in] for a 16.2hh horse). If he finds it too long or too short, adjust it a little at a time.

2 If the distance is correct your horse's feet will come down halfway between each pole.

3 Work over poles encourages a horse to flex his joints. Look at this horse's hocks. Raise the poles slightly to increase this flexion.

JUMPING

Incorporating lunge work over jumps enables you to see your horse's jumping style. If you spot any shortcomings in his technique, such as your horse dangles one foreleg, you can devise a programme to improve it.

Jumping like this also allows you to teach your horse to go forward and cope with any stride without being burdened by an out-of-balance rider. While for a horse, jumping on the lunge can improve confidence and address issues such as lack of impulsion and napping.

1 Start by popping over a small crosspole. Make sure that the jump wings are low so that it is easy to keep the lunge rein clear of them.

2 Move on to a bigger crosspole. Remember to keep the lunge rein contact without restricting your horse's head as he jumps.

3 If things go well make the fence into an upright. This experienced horse tucks up his front legs very neatly.

Lungeing

2:Groundwork in Practice

MASTERING TECHNIQUES

• Whatever the fence size, it is important, as when riding, to keep the horse coming towards it with impulsion but not speed. Rowan has the whip ready to give additional encouragement if necessary.

• A ground pole has been used to help the horse back off the fence a little rather than getting too close before take-off.

• Through all phases of the jump the handler must ensure that the horse has complete freedom to jump. When the horse is in flight the lunge rein has to allow for the movement of the horse's head and neck. However, control is required at all times.

• Side reins must not be used when jumping as they will restrict the horse's movement.

Even experienced horses can be wilful at times – this run-out shows how vital it is that the lunge rein can easily clear the jump wings without getting tangled in anything.

2: Groundwork in Practice

LUNGEING EXERCISES

LUNGEING WITH TWO REINS

Lungeing with two reins gives you more control over the horse's body and is useful as an introduction to long-reining. The lunge reins can be passed through rings on a lungeing roller, or, if your horse is saddled, run down the stirrups and secure them under the horse's belly with an additional

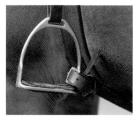

stirrup leather (above), so that they will not flap against his sides. Then thread the lunge reins through the stirrups.

TIP

- Use two reins to lunge your horse if he has a tendency to fall out through a shoulder or has problems coming through with the inside hind leg.

1 As with one-rein lungeing, it is important to maintain the triangle so that you have effective control.

2 As with riding it is important to keep an even and elastic contact on the reins; here you can see that there is more tension on the inside (red) rein.

3 It is important that the reins do not hang too low. They need to lie along the horse's body.

4 Take care to ensure that neither rein restricts forward movement of the horse. With the outside rein, it takes practise to ensure that you allow forward movement but do not let it go slack and slip below the buttock.

5 Use the outside rein to encourage or reinforce forward movement.

The Chambon, de Gogue and Pessoa are probably the most commonly used training aids. Any such aid must be used carefully, and preferably under instruction from someone with experience. Their purpose is to help a horse to move with more fluidity and engagement, but they can be detrimental when used incorrectly.

THE CHAMBON

The Chambon is only used for lungeing, never for riding. It brings about a lowered head carriage by applying pressure on the poll. The idea is to induce stretching in the head and neck. This in turn affects the muscles of the back and loins, encouraging the engagement of the hindquarters.

The Chambon consists of a divided rein that comes from the girth and passes between the forelegs and up through rings on a special fitting attached to the headpiece, behind the horse's ears. From there it goes down to the bit and is attached via clips.

It is initially fitted very loosely and the horse is worked in walk and then a slow trot until he is accustomed to how it feels. It can then be tightened gradually. Trot work is always done in a slow trot and must gradually be built up. No more than 20 minutes at a time is recommended.

DE GOGUE

The de Gogue came about as an extension of the Chambon and was designed so that it could be used in ridden work as well as for lungeing. It is useful for horses that are hollow-backed and have high head carriages as it offers them more freedom than side reins.

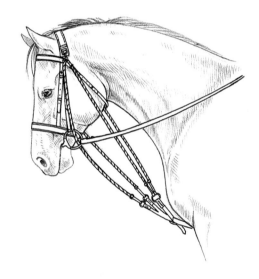

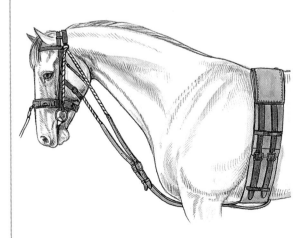

TIPS

- Be very careful when you use any device otherwise you could cause more problems.
- Consider your horse's musculature before any device is used. For instance, if his back muscles are in spasm then they cannot stretch, so using something like a Chambon, which is designed to stretch these muscles, will result in even more pain and spasm. Consult someone who is very experienced in using these gadgets if you think your horse needs this kind of work.

Lungeing

TRAINING AIDS

THE PESSOA

The Pessoa is useful for building and maintaining a horse's musculature. Developed by the showjumper Nelson Pessoa, it is good for horses whose muscles are functioning correctly as well as for those with back problems. However, as with other aids, it has to be used correctly. It consists of a roller and breeching lines. These are fixed to the roller and then go back to an elastic tensioner that sits around the horse's hindquarters. The tensioner is positioned behind the stifles, so that it encourages the horse to bring his hind legs further under his body. From the tensioner, lines run to the bit, via a ring on the roller and a pulley, and then through the fore legs to the roller again. There are four different positions and the horse must be worked progressively through each one in order to benefit from using this training aid. The Pessoa is designed so both ends of the horse are worked simultaneously and is good for helping a youngster find and develop his balance.

TIPS

- Muscle can be built very quickly using a Pessoa so it is essential that it is used correctly.
- Avoid over-tightening the lines and moving through the positions too quickly – these are common mistakes.
- Take care to introduce the tensioner gradually – otherwise your horse may become very frightened.
- Working a horse correctly in a Pessoa is a great way of allowing him to stretch without the weight of a rider on his back.

1 The first position encourages the horse to stretch down and work over his back. This position can also be used to warm up and cool down a horse. Horses are not worked in canter in this position.

2 The line goes through the pulleys attached to each bit ring and then between the front legs to attach to a ring on the roller. This set-up encourages the horse to lower his head. If he puts it too high, the line to the tensioner will act to send him on again.

3 The pulley system allows for fluid movement of the lines so that horse can easily take more contact on the rein.

4 As with other lungeing, the aim is to get the horse moving forwards easily, without leaning on the rein.

5 This horse is working forwards in a relaxed manner, stretching the muscles from his poll to tail.

2:Groundwork in Practice

6 This is the second position. The lines no longer go between the horse's forelegs but double back to attach to a ring on the roller, which means they are now in a similar position to normal side reins. Just as with side reins, the length of the line can be altered to suit each horse.

7 Here the second position is used for event horses at Novice level. When the horse's head is in the correct place the lines slacken, rewarding him.

8 The third position is used for horses working on the bit and in a collected frame. It is only suitable for advanced horses – if this position is used before the horse's training and musculature is sufficiently advanced it could cause problems.

9 This position should only be used by experienced trainers on experienced horses of intermediate and advanced level.

10 The most advanced position is only used for horses working at the top levels of dressage. The photo below shows how the ropes are crossed at the withers and attached to the opposite side.

FITTING THE TENSIONER

- Be careful when fitting the tensioner part of the Pessoa. Not all horses like the sensation of it around their quarters so introduce the feel of it carefully. The correct fit is shown below right.

- If the tensioner is fitted too tight (centre), then the effect is to 'scrunch up' the horse. He will not be rewarded for going forward and so tends to come back rather than move forward, adversely affecting his movement and muscular development.

- If the tensioner is fitted too low (left), the horse is likely to react by kicking out against it and there is the danger that he will get his leg caught over it if he does this.

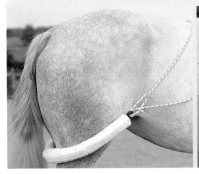

Case Study: A Green Horse

LUNGEING IN PRACTICE

Boris is a Thoroughbred who did not make it in the racing world. An inexperienced young woman bought him very cheaply at the sales while he was still quite young. She soon found he was too much for her and sold him on to an experienced home.

His new owner took Boris right back to basics, including lunge work, so that he could be taught to respond to the aids, to work more calmly and eventually to work in a rounder outline and strengthen his back. Soon Boris could walk, trot and canter in response to voice aids and in his own balance, without zooming around at great speed. The lunge work also helped to develop his muscles, without the burden of a rider on his back. Using transitions, spiralling in and out of circles and working over poles also helped him to develop suppleness, rhythm and balance. As he progressed, his owner started to work him over small jumps and helped him refine his jumping style before he was ridden.

His new owner found that working Boris on the lunge also helped her to build a good relationship with him before she got into the saddle. This was especially useful as Boris's time with his inexperienced owner had had the side effect of him losing respect for people and being rather dominant. Establishing control through the lunge line and voice also helped to improve his obedience and to diminish some other handling difficulties; for example leading him to the field, previously quite a problem, was no longer an issue.

Long-reining (long-lining)

WHY LONG-REIN?

Older members of the horse world will remember a time when long-reining was a vital part of a young horse's education. It was used to educate the horse so he understood the aids for going forwards, making turns and changes of direction and stopping, before a rider was put on board. In addition, young horses were long-reined around the countryside, on roads and tracks, so that they would become familiar with the sights and sounds they might meet when hacking. For a period long-reining seemed to go out of favour but recently it has undergone a revival with more people realizing its benefits.

Long-reining has many uses throughout a horse's life – it's invaluable for starting youngsters but can also be used to re-train older horses or to teach new skills, such as lateral movements and other more advanced work. You can practise a variety of riding techniques from the ground without upsetting his balance as well as use it to add variety to a horse's work. It is a valuable skill for every horseman to acquire.

Many of the 'new wave' of trainers, such as Kelly Marks and Michael Peace, do not lunge and therefore do not use lungeing as a precursor to long-reining. However, you may prefer to accustom your horse to lungeing before introducing the concept of long-reining. It does help if your horse responds to the voice aids, which he would learn through lungeing, and lungeing will also get him used to the feel of the lines along his side and around his buttocks.

Long-reining (long-lining)

LONG-REINING TECHNIQUES

Attach the long-reins to the bit as if they were normal reins. Usually they are then run either through the roller rings or through the stirrups, as for lungeing with two reins (page 118). However, until you are confident that your horse is happy, you may want to have the reins loose without going through the stirrups or roller rings; this will enable you to take control a little more easily if things go wrong.

Start on a circle as if you were lungeing using two reins. If your horse lunges but has never been long-reined introduce the second rein carefully – accustom him to the feel of the rein over his back and along his side. Ask a friend to stand beside him to reassure him. Be careful that the rein does not get caught under the his tail as this may well frighten him.

EQUIPMENT

- Headcollar or bridle. Young horses may be started off in a headcollar and then changed to a bridle when they understand the aids for turning and so on.
- Roller or saddle – the long-reins are fed through rings on the roller or though the stirrup irons, which are hanging down.
- Old stirrup leather to attach through both stirrup irons and fasten under the horse's belly. This is to keep the irons in position.
- Two long-reins of equal length – lunge lines are usually around 6m (20ft) long but extra long lines, 10m (30ft) long, can be bought.
- The handler should ideally wear a riding hat and gloves.

TIPS

- Long-rein a young horse in fields and along quiet tracks to educate him to the sights and sounds he may meet in the world.

- Use long-reining to vary your horse's normal training routine.

1 The reasonably long distance between the handler and horse shown here is suitable for a young horse. When long-reining, you need to be quick on your feet so that you can always stay with the horse's movement and are not pulling back on the lines, inhibiting forward movement.

2 With a safe, quiet and experienced horse, you can move closer in, giving more control. You must always be conscious of the horse's reactions and be careful when passing near the hindquarters.

3 The horse should take a light contact and move forwards without feeling strong in the handler's hands. Just as when riding, the horse is worked from the inside rein – acting where the rider's leg would be – to the outside rein. As you make changes of direction you will pass behind the horse but generally maintain an angle of 45 degrees to his hindquarters, where you will be safe but still able to drive him forwards.

Long-reining (long-lining)

LONG-REINING TECHNIQUES

Practise moves in walk before attempting them in trot. The secret is to plan ahead, be clear with your instructions, and keep everything flowing. Watch how you position yourself and, if necessary practise paying out and coiling up the long-reins.

1 This sequence shows a half circle to the right then a turn to the left.

2 Open the inside rein to indicate the direction of the turn.

3 As preparation for the change to the left rein, start to move over to the left.

4 Begin to open up the left rein.

2: Groundwork in Practice

5 The horse is now bending left...

6 ... and commences the half circle to the left.

7 Follow his movement and encourage him to step under himself more by flicking the inside rein along his side where the rider's leg would be. Time the flick to occur as he is about to move his inside leg forward.

8 Complete the half circle before continuing with other exercises, such as making changes of rein, circles and serpentines, all of which add interest for the horse.

Case Study: A Neglected Horse

LONG-REINING IN PRACTICE

When she bought a new horse, Sophie asked her friend Jenny to help with him. It soon became clear that Jet had quite a few problems. He was in poor condition, had very little muscle, could not even walk straight and didn't seem aware of his own limbs. Jenny suggested that Sophie get Jet checked over by a vet and ask one of the feed companies for advice on feeding him.

Some weeks later Jenny felt that Jet could now cope with some work, but not under saddle. She showed Sophie how to long-rein and allowed Sophie practise on one of her own horses – he was an old hand at being long-reined. When she was competent, Sophie moved on to long-reining Jet, initially working him on straight lines to aid symmetrical muscle development. She long-reined him around the arena at first until she was confident with her control, turning and stopping. Then she moved on to long-reining around the farm and eventually on quieter roads and tracks. At this point she was able to make use of the many small hills in the area, long-reining Jet up inclines to help build his hindquarter muscles.

Back in the arena, she introduced various arrangements of poles so that Jet became more aware of his legs and where he was putting them. This helped his muscle strength, flexibility and co-ordination.

Jet is now a different horse, in good condition and well aware of his body. He enjoys all kinds of work, including competitions, and long-reining sessions are still a regular part of his routine.

In-hand work

2:Groundwork in Practice

Working horses in-hand has been an integral part of horsemanship for centuries but is often a neglected area today. However, there are many advantages to be gained from acquiring this skill, which can be introduced to horses of any age, regardless of their history.

THE BENEFITS

In-hand work:

- develops the horse's musculature
- accustoms the horse to vocal and touch commands
- teaches the horse a variety of movements and makes it easier for him to then execute the movements under saddle
- builds a horse's confidence and self-esteem
- adds variety to the horse's work programme
- enables a rider to work a horse in a short time – useful when riding is not an option
- provides discipline for the horse
- develops a deeper relationship between horse and handler

In-hand work

PREPARATION AND BASIC SKILLS

Teach your horse to lunge so that he is used to going forwards and then introduce the side reins to encourage him to work in a shape. Then you can use a combination of lungeing and in-hand work to help him develop his muscles, so that he can lift his back and shoulders, and improve his topline. Our models are from Turville Valley Stud, where they use Portuguese training methods, including top reins (see opposite) as well as side reins. The horses here are not worked long and low. Instead, they are taught to carry themselves and to work in a good shape from the start. A gentle swishing of their tails as they walk reveals how supple they are.

1 This is a Portuguese-style lungeing cavesson. It has a metal noseband that the horse has to learn to respect. A conventional lungeing cavesson is not used at the stud as they feel it can cause pinching.

2 The roller is made as one piece of equipment so that it can be put on over the saddle without having to disconnect the side reins. It is based upon a Portuguese design.

3 To work successfully in-hand your horse should be used to responding to your voice, body language and whip while being lunged.

4 If a youngster is being lunged at the stud two people are used; one holds the lunge rein while the other is positioned on the inside of the circle, ready with a whip to encourage the horse to keep moving on. Starting a young horse off in this way reduces the likelihood of him stopping, whizzing around or coming in towards the handler.

5 The top rein is added to help with the carriage of the head...

6 ... and the horse is lunged with both side and top reins fitted.

In-hand work

2: Groundwork in Practice

WHIP-WISE

Working in-hand involves using a whip at specific points:

- where the rider's leg would be used to generate impulsion
- on the hocks to ask the horse to step under more or to increase the activity (when teaching a movement such as piaffe)
- on the horse's forearm to extend and lighten the action of the fore leg
- on the chest to slow or stop the horse

EQUIPMENT

- Leather lungeing cavesson with a long lead rope; alternatively a bridle
- Schooling whip
- Outdoor arena or other suitable area to work in

1 Stroke the horse while holding the whip in the hand that is making contact with him. Then stroke him with part of the whip. Start off at the shoulder area and gradually work over his body.

2 Little by little use more of the whip so that eventually the horse accepts being touched all over with it. Before you attempt any in-hand work he must be totally relaxed with this whip – if he isn't or is anxious in any way you will not be able to progress effectively.

3 During in-hand work, touching the whip across the chest will encourage the horse to stop or slow down.

In-hand work

1 At Turville Valley Stud, signals that will eventually be communicated with the whip are taught using vocal commands that coincide with a whip movement. Here the whip is applied on the loins – a signal to stop.

2 The horses are taught to accept the use of the whip on the neck as a slowing aid. A long whip is used so that no areas of the horse's body are out of reach.

3 Rhythmic taps on either side of the croup may be used when teaching piaffe in-hand.

4 Touching the horse with the whip in the girth area is used to simulate the rider's leg aid.

5 A horse that is accustomed to the feel of the whip signals, can be asked to step around in either direction. This walk turn on the forehand helps to build strength over the loins, the weakest part of the back.

On occasion a shorter birch stick is used instead of the lunge whip.

When working a horse in-hand with a bridle, the reins are held over his neck. This allows them to be used as if a rider were on board, the inside rein asking for flexion, the outside rein being supporting and preventing too much flexion.

In-hand work

Once you have practised the basics and can move, stop and direct the horse around on a circle, working on both reins, try other work. When you start schooling in-hand, you will soon come to appreciate the benefits to your own dexterity in working the horse from both sides.

2 Teach your horse to do rein back – look for definite steps, made straight back.

1 As you and your horse progress, you can go from one movement to another, for example from half-pass to walk turn on the forehand to half-pass again.

3 Travers (hindquarters in), shown from ground level and above, can also be taught in-hand.

In-hand work

2: Groundwork in Practice

PIAFFE

Horses are athletes, and in-hand work helps to develop their athleticism and suppleness. Piaffe requires the horse to really engage his hindquarters and lighten his forehand, moving his legs in diagonal pairs so that he appears to trot on the spot. This requires great collection, with the horse having to lower his croup and increase the flexion in his hocks and knees to give clear suspension to the movement.

1 Part of the preparation for teaching a horse to piaffe can be done in-hand. The horse is taught to bring his hindquarters underneath him.

2 The whip on his hind legs indicates that he is to bring them further under him. Remember to praise your horse for his efforts.

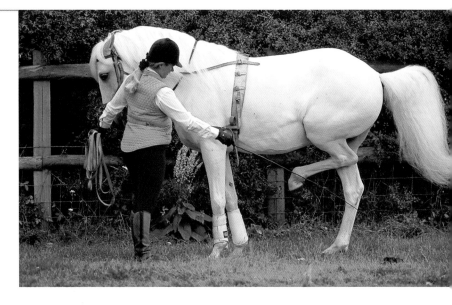

3 Quick and light touches with the whip on the hind legs encourages him to flex and lift each hind leg in turn.

④ By teaching the horse to piaffe in-hand first, the job of the rider is made easier. All of the work that was done in-hand can be repeated with a rider on board so that the horse makes the connection between the in-hand signals and the aids given by the rider.

ADVANCED SKILLS – SPANISH WALK

2: Groundwork in Practice

SPANISH WALK

The Spanish walk looks striking and has the practical value of encouraging the horse to really use his shoulders. In fact, it has beneficial effects for all horses, whether working on the flat or over fences. To perform it, a horse also needs to be well balanced and be truly engaged behind.

TIPS

- All horses and ponies can benefit from in-hand work. Older horses can be helped to overcome their stiffness – but remember that they will not be able to work to the same degree as younger horses. Only work for short periods of time, irrespective of the horse's age.

- Teaching your horse to flex his neck in both directions (below) will help to ease any resistance in this area and make it easier for him to do in-hand and ridden work.

1 The handler uses the whip to encourage the horse to lift a foreleg ....

2 ... and then to increase the stretch of the fore leg, as preparation for Spanish walk.

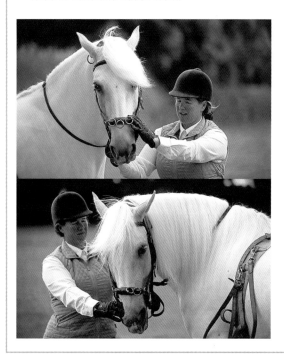

3 Lifting the leg in this way increases the use of the shoulder.

④ Work to strengthen the shoulders pays off when the horse is asked to do the Spanish walk with a rider.

Working on yourself

PILATES

Your posture is just as important when working a horse from the ground as it is when you are riding. A good posture makes a statement to the horse when riding as you can maintain a balanced, upright but relaxed position so that it is easy for him to carry you. When working from the ground, your posture will also affect your horse. Imagine trying to long-rein with a crooked body. This would inevitably have effects upon the rein aids you were transmitting to the horse.

The exercise programme called Pilates helps to improve your core muscles (your trunk) to give you greater stability and more control over your body. As you will realize from reading about the different types of groundwork, being able to control your body and mind is crucial to your success. It is also valuable for you as a rider as it strengthens the muscles that control the position of your shoulders and neck and, importantly, the muscles around your stomach, which work with your pelvic floor and your back muscles, to support your spine. By re-training these muscles, it helps you to achieve a better posture and spinal alignment. As a result, riders who practise Pilates find it easier to maintain a correct position and to apply the aids correctly.

Joseph Pilates was born in Germany in 1880. A frail child, he turned to various physical fitness programmes in order to improve his health but eventually developed his own workout system. After the First World War, he emigrated to the USA and moved to New York, where he opened a fitness studio in the same building that housed the New York City Ballet. Leading dancers came to him, soon followed by sportsmen, actors, and the rich and famous.

Among the reasons for Pilates' popularity are that it builds strength without bulk, enhances flexibility and allows the body to work efficiently with minimal effort and no tension.

Each Pilates exercise incorporates the following elements:

- Deep breathing using the whole of the lungs
- Relaxation and body awareness leading to a release of muscle tension
- Centering – building a strong centre or girdle of strength to support the trunk
- Alignment – correcting muscle imbalances
- Flowing movement so there is no damage to muscles or joints
- Stamina
- Co-ordination
- Concentration

Classes in Pilates are now widely available and you shouldn't have difficulty in locating one in your area.

NEURO-LINGUISTIC PROGRAMMING

There are times when working with a horse leads to frustration as you try to get him to do something and the result is anything but the desired response. There can be several reasons for this and it is important that you do not let frustration or temper get the better of you. Being able to control the responses you have to situations is a valuable skill and is something you can learn via NLP.

NLP brings together three areas:

- Neurology – the mind and how we think
- Linguistics – the language we use and how it affects us
- Programming – how we sequence our actions to achieve goals

Through studying NLP, you can get the power to make changes in your attitudes and behaviour thus affecting your relationship with your horse. It is also an aid to help riders control their nerves and achieve their goals.

CASE STUDY

Lucy is a competent rider who has owned several horses and taken part in all horse sports. Until recently she has competed regularly but a change of horse resulted in a loss of confidence. Lucy's previous horses had all been onward-bound confident jumpers, prepared to take her into the fences, even when she felt apprehensive. Her new horse is much younger than the others and needs Lucy to ride him more positively. If she is not 110% positive then he stops. This has been happening more often, especially in competitions, and Lucy's confidence has begun to ebb away.

A friend suggested that Lucy try a day course in NLP specifically aimed at riders. She went along to the dismounted course and to her surprise found that the exercises enabled her to sort out her somewhat confused feelings. Through asking questions, the course leader helped Lucy to realize how she was allowing her mind to work against her. Every time they entered the jumping ring, she had a huge image of herself and her horse refusing at a fence. When this actually happened, Lucy felt disappointed and ashamed.

On the NLP course, Lucy learned to 'shrink' the bad picture and lock it away, replacing it with a positive image of her horse jumping fences cleanly. She was encouraged to recreate the feeling of her horse jumping well over a fence, acknowledging the joy it gave her, the smell of the grass and the horse – all the scents associated with a good day – and to remember the feeling of being presented with rosettes, of doing the lap of honour, of praising her horse for doing well. Then, through a process known as anchoring, she was able to plant the good image in her memory and learn how to recall it at a moment's notice.

The day course also helped her to realize what motivated her to compete and this helped her to change the way she thought about making a mistake. Instead of it being something shameful, Lucy has learned to see a mistake as an opportunity to learn and to improve.

The good news is that Lucy is putting her new-found mental skills to use and is competing again. Her horse is jumping much better as Lucy is more positive and confident. When they do make a mistake, she is better able to deal with it and overall both are growing in confidence.

THE TRAINERS (in order of appearance!)

Further Information & Index

LESLEY BAYLEY
Can be contacted through
the publishers or as follows:
lesley.bayley@virgin.net
Tel: 01572 787257

LESLEY BAYLEY is a qualified
Equine Muscle Release Therapy
practitioner. She is former
editor of *Your Horse* magazine
and author of numerous
equestrian books including
seven for David & Charles.

MONTY ROBERTS
www.montyroberts.com

**INTELLIGENT
HORSEMANSHIP**
Tel: 01488 71300
kelly@montyroberts.co.uk
www.intelligenthorsemanship.co.uk

KELLY MARKS orginated the
Monty Roberts educational
courses worldwide and also
founded the Intelligent
Horsemanship Association.

MARK RASHID
www.markrashid.com

MARK RASHID considers the
horse's point of view and
pursues quiet and effective
ways of training horses.

DAN FRANKLIN
www.equine-
communication.com
Tel: 01332 280563
Mobile: 07929 917418

DAN FRANKLIN travels
worldwide teaching people to
communicate with their
horses intuitively.

PAT PARELLI
www.parelli.com

**PARELLI NATURAL
HORSEMANSHIP**
UK Savvy Centre,

Wilson Farm, Rackenford,
Tiverton, Devon, EX16 8ED
Tel: 01884 881254
www.parelli.biz

INGELA SAINSBURY is a Level
3* instructor with Parelli
Natural Horsemanship.

THINK EQUUS
Michael Peace, PO Box 230,
Kidlington, Oxfordshire,
OX5 2TU
Tel: 01865 842806
www.thinkequus.com

MICHAEL PEACE founded
Think Equus, a non-
confrontational approach to
training horses.

POSITIVE HORSE MAGIC
Ross and Heather Simpson,
Natural Animal Centre,
Penhil, Trawsmawr,
Nr Carmarthen,
Carmarthenshire,
Wales SA33 6ND
Tel: 0870 991 3334
www.naturalanimalcentre.com

ROSS SIMPSON and his wife
Heather run the Natural
Animal Centre combining
positive reinforcement
training techniques and horse
psychology in their work.

TTEAM
UK TTEAM Centre, Tilley
Farm, Farmborough, Bath,
Somerset, BA2 0AB.

Tel: 01761 471182
www.tilleyfarm.co.uk
US office PO Box 3793, Santa
Fé, New Mexico, 87501-3793
www.lindatellingtonjones.com

SARAH FISHER is the highest
qualified TTEAM practitioner
in the UK and runs a holistic
treatment centre for animals.

ROWAN INGE
Can be contacted through
Lesley Bayley (see above)

ROWAN INGE produces
horses for all disciplines,
specialising in lungeing and
long-reining techniques.

TURVILLE VALLEY STUD
Turville Valley Stud, Turville,
Nr Henley-on-Thames, Oxon,
RG9 6QU
Tel: 01491 638338
www.turvillevalleystud.co.uk

TURVILLE VALLEY STUD is a
classical riding centre run by
Diane Thurman-Baker and
Angela Fois. They specialize in
breeding and training Lusitanos.

Index